S0-BUB-899

COLD BLOOD II

COLD BLOOD II

EDITED BY PETER SELLERS

MOSAIC PRESS
Oakville – New York – London

CANADIAN CATALOGUING IN PUBLICATION DATA

Cold blood II

ISBN 0-88962-417-8 (bound) ISBN 0-88962-416-X (pbk.)

1. Detective and mystery stories, Canadian (English).*
I. Sellers, Peter, 1956-   .

PS823.D4C62 1989   C813'.0872'08   C89-094765-1
PR9197.35.D48C62 1989

No part of this book may be reproduced or transmitted in any form, by any means, electronic or mechanical, including photocopying and recording in-formation   storage and retrieval systems, without permission in writing from the publisher, except by a reviewer who may quote brief passages in a review.

Published by MOSAIC PRESS, P.O. Box 1032, Oakville, Ontario, L6J 5E9, Canada. Offices and warehouse at 1252 Speers Road, Units # 1&2, Oakville, Ontario, L6L 5N9, Canada.

Mosaic Press acknowledges the assistance of the Canada Council and the Ontario Arts Council in support of its publishing programme.

"The Devil Made Me Do It" copyright, 1989 by Mel D. Ames
"Year of the Dragon" copyright, 1989 by Tony Aspler
"One More Story To Tell" copyright, 1988 by William Bankier
"That Was No Lady" copyright, 1989 by Jack Barnao
"A Tale of a Tub" copyright, 1989 by Charlotte Macleod. Reprinted by permis-sion of International Creative Management, Inc. New York. All rights reserved.
"Safe As Houses" copyright, 1989 by Elaine Mitchell Matlow
"Sudden Withdrawal" copyright, 1989 by John North
"Good Night, Mrs. Calabash, Wherever You Are" copyright, 1989 by Sara Plews
"Dark Shoes" copyright, 1989 by Jas. R. Petrin
"Fan Mail" copyright, 1989 by Peter Robinson
"Somewhere They Can't Find Me" copyright, 1989 by Peter Sellers
"A Question of Proof" copyright, 1989 by Ted Wood
"Hephaestus" copyright, 1989 by Eric Wright
"Introduction" copyright, 1989 by Peter Sellers

Design by Rita Vogel
Typeset by Bambam Type & Graphics
Printed and Bound in Canada.

ISBN 0-88962-416-X PAPER
ISBN 0-88962-417-8 CLOTH

MOSAIC PRESS:
In Canada:
        MOSAIC PRESS, 1252 Speers Road, Units # 1&2, Oakville, Ontario L6J 5N9, Canada. P.O. Box 1032, Oakville, Ontario L6J 5E9

In the United States:
        Distributed by Kampmann & Co., 226 West 26th Street, New York, N.Y., 10001, USA, or Riverrun Press Inc., 1170 Broadway, Suite 807, New York, N.Y., 10001, U.S.A.,

In the U.K.:
        John Calder (Publishers) Ltd., 18 Brewer Street, London, W1R 4A5, England.

For my mother and father,
who taught me the value of stories

TABLE OF CONTENTS

Fan Mail
Peter Robinson 11

That Was No Lady
Jack Barnao 29

Somewhere They Can't Find Me
Peter Sellers 41

Sudden Withdrawal
John North 53

Hephaestus
Eric Wright 63

A Tale of a Tub
Charlotte MacLeod 73

The Devil Made Me Do It
Mel D. Ames 85

Goodnight, Mrs. Calabash, Wherever You Are
Sara Plews 111

A Question of Proof
Ted Wood 119

Safe As Houses
Elaine Mitchell Matlow 127

Dark Shoes
Jas. R. Petrin 137

One More Story To Tell
William Bankier 161

Year of the Dragon
Tony Aspler 177

INTRODUCTION

by Peter Sellers

The short crime story has fallen on hard times. Short fiction in every form has suffered at the hands of television and video, but perhaps crime fiction has fared worst of all. Today, collections such as this one are the only market for short crime fiction to be found, except for two major national magazines and a handful of subscription-only enthusiast publications.

If the history of the short crime story were different, this might not be so unfortunate. But, as it is, the whole crime and mystery genre began with the short story form. When Edgar Allan Poe published the first of his three C. Auguste Dupin stories "The Murders in the Rue Morgue" in Graham's Magazine in 1841, he started a new literary tradition which was to grow to a richness beyond even his wildest dreams. Through that first story and its successors, "The Mystery of Marie Roget", serialized in Snowden's Ladies' Companion in November and December 1842 and February 1843, and "The Purloined Letter" published in the Gift, in December 1844, Poe introduced many of the conventions which today virtually define the genre. The private detective of great intuition. The Boswell-like narrator. The locked room murder. The "how-did-he-solve-it" as well as the whodunit.

If Poe's three tales began the field, Conan Doyle made it popular. His Sherlock Holmes stories gave mystery fiction a respectability and an icon which it has never lost. Even people who've never read any mystery stories at all know of Holmes and Baker Street.

In North America, the tradition was similar. The early part of the century saw the rise of crime fighting heroes from the pages of the penny dreadfuls to the dime novels to the pulps. There were, between the late 1920's and early forties some 200 crime pulps alone. Their pages were full of the exploits of private detectives like Sam Spade and the Continental Op, Race Williams and Philip Marlowe. And, while their methods were frequently quite different from the more genteel and cerebral British private investigators, their popularity was the same. From the yellowing pulps, the detectives moved on, taking many of the finer writers with them and they found a new home as paperback staples in the forties and fifties, as the pulps which had spawned them began to dwindle and die. And that was the beginning of the end of the glory days of the short crime story.

In Canada, the tradition of short crime fiction is as rich as anywhere else. Names from the past include Grant Allen and Robert Barr, whose "The Absent-Minded Coterie" is considered one of the finest short mystery stories ever. And for the past twenty-five years, writers such as William Bankier, James Powell and Mel D. Ames have been exporting Canadian crime fiction which, especially in the cases of Bankier's popular Baytown stories and Powell's Mountie hero Maynard Bullock, is unabashedly Canadian.

What COLD BLOOD hopes to create is a forum for even more Canadian writers of short crime fiction. From the well known names such as Eric Wright, Ted Wood and Charlotte Macleod to the new and unknown. Running the gamut from stories of pure suspense to pulpy action stories to tales of what Poe called ratiocination.

In this second collection of entirely original material you'll find yourself in the eerie gloom of a tattoo parlour as a Chinese master decorates a sailor's back in Tony Aspler's "Year of the Dragon". You'll spend a week's dream holiday in the sun which Eric Wright turns into a nightmare for the characters in "Hephaestus". You'll visit both the violent, chaotic world of professional wrestling in Mel D. Ames' "The Devil Made Me Do It" and the precise order of a downtown bank in John North's "Sudden Withdrawal". You'll read about a killing in real estate in Elaine Mitchell Matlow's "Safe as Houses" and you'll experience the beauty and danger to be found in Ontario's northern wilderness in "That Was No Lady" by Jack Barnao.

The style of each story is unique. The only constant is the talent of the storytellers.

Short crime fiction may not be as widely read as it once was. But, as this collection proves, it's certainly every bit as well written.

Peter Sellers
Toronto
January, 1989

Peter Robinson

Born in Yorkshire in 1950, Peter Robinson came
to Canada in 1974. He lives in Toronto where he
writes and teaches. His first novel, *Gallows
View*, introduced Cheif Inpsector Alan Banks,
and was short listed for both the John Creasey
Award in England and the Crime Writers of
Canada's Arthur Ellis Award for Best first Novel.
A second Banks novel, *A Dedicated Man*, was
published in 1988 and was also an Ellis nominee.
His third, *A Necessary End*, has just been published. "Fan Mail" is Robinson's first published
short story.

FAN MAIL

by Peter Robinson

The letter arrived one sunny Thursday morning in August, along with a Visa bill and a royalty statement. Dennis Quilley carried the mail out to the deck of his Beaches home, stopping by the kitchen on the way to pour himself a gin and tonic. He had already been writing for three hours straight, and he felt he deserved a drink.

First he looked at the amount of the royalty cheque, then he put aside the Visa bill and picked up the letter carefully, as if he were a forensic expert investigating it for prints. Postmarked Toronto, and dated four days earlier, it was addressed in a small, precise hand and looked as if it had been written with a fine-nibbed calligraphic pen. But the postal code was different; that had been hurriedly scrawled in with a ball-point. Whoever it was, Quilley thought, had probably got his name from the telephone directory and had then looked up the code in the post office just before mailing.

Pleased with his deductions, Quilley opened the letter. Written in the same neat and mannered hand as the address, it said:

> Dear Mr Quilley,
>
> Please forgive me for writing to you at home like this. I know you must be very busy, and it is inexcusable of me to intrude on your valuable time. Believe me, I would not do so if I could think of any other way.
>
> I have been a great fan of your work for many years now. As a collector of mysteries, too, I also have first editions of all your books. From what I have read, I know you are a clever man, and, I hope, just the man to help me with my problem.
>
> For the past twenty years, my wife has been making my life a misery. I put up with her for the sake of the children, but now they have all gone to live their own lives. I have asked her for a divorce, but she just laughed in my face. I have decided, finally, that the only way out is to kill her, and that is why I am seeking your advice.
>
> You may think this is insane of me, especially saying it in a letter, but it is just a measure of my desperation. I would

quite understand it if you went straight to the police, and I am sure they would find me and punish me. Believe me, I've thought about it. Even that would be preferable to the misery I must suffer day after day.

If you can find it in your heart to help a devoted fan in his hour of need, please meet me on the roof lounge of the Park Plaza Hotel on Wednesday, August 19 at two p.m. I have taken the afternoon off work and will wait longer if for any reason you are delayed. Don't worry, I will recognize you easily from your photo on the dust-jackets of your books.

Yours, in hope,
A Fan.

The letter slipped from Quilley's hand. He couldn't believe what he'd just read. He was a mystery writer -- he specialized in devising ingenious murders -- but for someone to assume that he did the same in real life was absurd. Could it be a practical joke?

He picked up the letter and read through it again. The man's whining tone and cliched style seemed sincere enough, and the more Quilley thought about it, the more certain he became that none of his friends was sick enough to play such a joke.

Assuming that it was real then, what should he do? His impulse was to crumple up the letter and throw it away. But should he go to the police? No. That would be a waste of time. The real police were a terribly dull and literal-minded lot. They would probably think he was seeking publicity.

He found that he had screwed up the sheet of paper in his fist, and he was just about to toss it aside when he changed his mind. Wasn't there another option? Go. Go and meet the man. Find out more about him. Find out if he was genuine. Surely there would be no obligation in that? All he had to do was turn up at the Park Plaza at the appointed time and see what happened.

Quilley's life was fine -- no troublesome woman to torment him, plenty of money (mostly from American sales), a beautiful lakeside cottage near Huntsville, a modicum of fame, the esteem of his peers -- but it had been rather boring of late. Here was an opportunity for adventure of a kind. Besides, he might get a story idea out of the meeting. Why not go and see?

He finished his drink and smoothed the letter on his knee. He had to smile at that last bit. No doubt the man would recognize him from his book-jacket photo, but it was an old one and had been retouched in the first place. His cheeks had filled out a bit since then, and his thinning hair had acquired a sprinkling of grey. Still, he thought, he was a handsome man for fifty: handsome, clever and successful.

Smiling, he picked up both letter and envelope and went back to the kitchen in search of matches. There must be no evidence.

*   *   *   *   *

Over the next few days, Quilley hardly gave a thought to the mysterious letter. As usual in summer, he divided his time between writing in Toronto, where he found the city worked as a stimulus, and weekends at the cottage. There, he walked in the woods, chatted to locals in the lodge, swam in the clear lake and idled around getting a tan. Evenings, he would open a bottle of chardonnay, reread P.G. Wodehouse and listen to Bach. It was an ideal life: quiet, solitary, independent.

When Wednesday came, though, he drove downtown, parked in the multi-storey garage at Cumberland and Avenue Road, then walked to the Park Plaza. It was another hot day. The tourists were out in force across Bloor Street by the Royal Ontario Museum, many of them Americans from Buffalo, Rochester or Detroit: the men in loud checked shirts photographing everything in sight, their wives in tight shorts looking tired and thirsty.

Quilley took the elevator up to the nineteenth floor and wandered through the bar, an olde-worlde place with deep armchairs and framed reproductions of old Colonial scenes on the walls. It was busier than usual, and even though the windows were open, the smoke bothered him. He walked out onto the roof lounge and scanned the faces. Within moments he noticed someone looking his way. The man paused for just a split-second, perhaps to translate the dust-jacket photo into reality, then beckoned Quilley over with raised eyebrows and a twitch of the head.

The man rose to shake hands, then sat down again, glancing around to make sure nobody had paid the two of them undue attention. He was short and thin, with sandy hair and a pale grey complexion, as if he had just come out of hospital. He wore wire-rimmed glasses and had a habit of rolling his tongue around in his mouth when he wasn't talking.

"First of all, Mr Quilley," the man said, raising his glass, "may I say how honoured I am to meet you." He spoke with a pronounced English accent.

Quilley inclined his head. "I'm flattered, Mr...er...?"

"Peplow, Frank Peplow."

"Yes...Mr Peplow. But I must admit I'm puzzled by your letter."

A waiter in a burgundy jacket came over to take Quilley's order. He asked for an Amstel.

Peplow paused until the waiter was out of earshot. "Puzzled?"

"What I mean is," Quilley went on, struggling for the right

words, "whether you were serious or not, whether you really do want to --"

Peplow leaned forward. Behind the lenses, his pale blue eyes looked sane enough. "I assure you, Mr Quilley, that I was, that I *am* entirely serious. That woman is ruining my life and I can't allow it to go on any longer."

Speaking about her brought little spots of red to his cheeks. Quilley held his hand up. "All right, I believe you. I suppose you realize I should have gone to the police?"

"But you didn't."

"I could have. They might be here, watching us."

Peplow shook his head. "Mr Quilley, if you won't help, I'd even welcome prison. Don't think I haven't realized that I might get caught, that no murder is perfect. All I want is a chance. It's worth the risk."

The waiter returned with Quilley's drink, and they both sat in silence until he had gone. Quilley was intrigued by this drab man sitting opposite him, a man who obviously didn't even have the imagination to dream up his own murder plot. "What do you want from me?" he asked.

"I have no right to ask anything of you, I understand that," Peplow said. "I have absolutely nothing to offer in return. I'm not rich. I have no savings. I suppose all I want really is advice, encouragement."

"If I were to help," Quilley said. "*If* I were to help, then I'd do nothing more than offer advice. Is that clear?"

Peplow nodded. "Does that mean you will?"

"If I can."

And so Dennis Quilley found himself helping to plot the murder of a woman he'd never met with a man he didn't even particularly like. Later, when he analyzed his reasons for playing along, he realized that that was exactly what he had been doing -- playing. It had been a game, a cerebral puzzle, just like thinking up a plot for a book, and he never, at first, gave a thought to real murder, real blood, real death.

Peplow took a handkerchief from his top pocket and wiped the thin film of sweat from his brow. "You don't know how happy this makes me, Mr Quilley. At last, I have a chance. My life hasn't amounted to much, and I don't suppose it ever will. But at least I might find some peace and quiet in my final years. I'm not a well man." He placed one hand solemnly over his chest. "Ticker. Not fair, is it? I've never smoked, I hardly drink, and I'm only fifty-three. But the doctor has promised me a few years yet if I live right. All I want is to be left alone with my books and my garden."

"Tell me about your wife," Quilley prompted.

Peplow's expression darkened. "She's a cruel and selfish

woman," he said. "And she's messy, she never does anything around the place. Too busy watching those damn soap-operas on television day and night. She cares about nothing but her own comfort, and she never overlooks an opportunity to nag me or taunt me. If I try to escape to my collection, she mocks me and calls me dull and boring. I'm not even safe from her in my garden. I realize I have no imagination, Mr Quilley, and perhaps even less courage, but even a man like me deserves some peace in his life, don't you think?"

Quilley had to admit that the woman really did sound awful -- worse than any he had known, and he had met some shrews in his time. He had never had much use for women, except for occasional sex in his younger days. Even that had become sordid, and now he stayed away from them as much as possible. He found, as he listened, that he could summon up remarkable sympathy for Peplow's position.

"What do you have in mind?" he asked.

"I don't really know. That's why I wrote to you. I was hoping you might be able to help with some ideas. Your books ... you seem to know so much."

"In my books," Quilley said, "the murderer always gets caught."

"Well, yes," said Peplow, "of course. But that's because the genre demands it, isn't it? I mean, your Inspector Baldry is much smarter than any real policeman. I'm sure if you'd made him a criminal, he would always get away."

There was no arguing with that, Quilley thought. "How do you want to do it?" he asked. "A domestic accident? Electric shock, say? Gadget in the bathtub? She must have a hair curler or a dryer?"

Peplow shook his head, eyes tightly closed. "Oh no," he whispered, "I couldn't. I couldn't do anything like that. No more than I could bear the sight of her blood."

"How's her health?"

"Unfortunately," said Peplow, "she seems obscenely robust."

"How old is she?"

"Forty-nine."

"Any bad habits?"

"Mr Quilley, my wife has nothing *but* bad habits. The only thing she won't tolerate is drink, for some reason, and I don't think she has other men -- though that's probably because nobody will have her."

"Does she smoke?"

"Like a chimney."

Quilley shuddered. "How long?"

"Ever since she was a teenager, I think. Before I met her."

"Does she exercise?"

"Never."

"What about her weight, her diet?"

"Well, you might not call her fat, but you'd be generous in saying she was full-figured. She eats too much junk food. I've always said that. And eggs. She loves bacon and eggs for breakfast. And she's always stuffing herself with cream-cakes and tarts."

"Hmmm," said Quilley, taking a sip of Amstel. "She sounds like a prime candidate for a heart attack."

"But it's me who —" Peplow stopped as comprehension dawned. "I see. Yes, I see. You mean one could be *induced*?"

"Quite. Do you think you could manage that?"

"Well, I could if I didn't have to be there to watch. But I don't know how."

"Poison."

"I don't know anything about poison."

"Never mind. Give me a few days to look into it. I'll give you advice, remember, but that's as far as it goes."

"Understood."

Quilley smiled. "Good. Another beer?"

"No, I'd better not. She'll be able to smell this on my breath and I'll be in for it already. I'd better go."

Quilley looked at his watch. Two-thirty. He could have done with another Amstel, but he didn't want to stay there by himself. Besides, at half past three it would be time to meet his agent at the Windsor Arms, and there he would have the opportunity to drink as much as he wanted. To pass the time, he could browse through the magazines and imported newspapers in the Reader's Den. "Fine," he said, "I'll go down with you."

Outside on the hot, busy street, they shook hands and agreed to meet in a week's time on the back patio of the Madison Avenue Pub. It wouldn't do to be seen together twice in the same place.

Quilley stood on the corner of Bloor and Avenue Road among the camera-clicking tourists and watched Peplow walk off towards the St George subway station. Now that their meeting was over and the spell was broken, he wondered again what the hell he was doing helping this pathetic little man. It certainly wasn't altruism. Perhaps the challenge appealed to him; after all, people climb mountains just because they're there.

And then there was Peplow's mystery collection. There was just a chance that it might contain an item of great interest to Quilley, and that Peplow might be grateful enough to part with it.

Wondering how to approach the subject at their next meeting, Quilley wiped the sweat from his brow with the back of his hand and walked towards the bookshop.

* * * * *

Atropine, hyoscyamine, belladonna....Quilley flipped through Dreisbach's *Handbook of Poisoning* one evening at the cottage. Poison seemed to have gone out of fashion these days, and he had only used it in one of his novels, about six years ago. That had been the old stand-by, cyanide, with its familiar smell of bitter almonds that he had so often read about but never experienced. The small black handbook had sat on his shelf gathering dust ever since.

Writing a book, of course, one could generally skip over the problems of acquiring the stuff -- give the killer a job as a pharmacist or in a hospital dispensary, for example. In real life, getting one's hands on poison might prove more difficult.

So far, he had read through the sections on agricultural poisons, household hazards and medicinal poisons. The problem was that whatever Peplow used had to be easily available. Prescription drugs were out. Even if Peplow could persuade a doctor to give him barbiturates, for example, the prescription would be on record and any death in the household would be regarded as suspicious. Barbiturates wouldn't do, anyway, and nor would such common products as paint thinner, insecticides and weed killers -- they didn't reproduce the symptoms of a heart attack.

Near the back of the book was a list of poisonous plants that shocked Quilley by its sheer length. He hadn't known just how much deadliness there was lurking in fields, gardens and woods. Rhubarb leaves contained oxalic acid, for example, and caused nausea, vomiting and diarrhea. The bark, wood, leaves or seeds of the yew had a similar effect. Boxwood leaves and twigs caused convulsions; celandine could bring about a coma; hydrangeas contained cyanide; and laburnums brought on irregular pulse, delirium, twitching and unconsciousness. And so the list went on -- lupins, mistletoe, sweet peas, rhododendron -- a poisoner's delight. Even the beautiful poinsettia, which brightened up so many Toronto homes each Christmas, could cause gastroenteritis. Most of these plants were easy to get hold of, and in many cases the active ingredients could be extracted simply by soaking or boiling in water.

It wasn't long before Quilley found what he was looking for. Beside "Oleander", the note read, "See *digitalis*, 374." And there it was, set out in detail. Digitalis occurred in all parts of the common foxglove, which grew on waste ground and woodland slopes, and flowered from June to September. Acute poisoning would bring about death from ventricular fibrillation. No doctor would consider an autopsy if Peplow's wife appeared to die of a heart attack, given her habits, especially if Peplow fed her a few smaller doses first to establish the symptoms.

Quilley set aside the book. It was already dark outside, and the downpour that the humid, cloudy day had been promising had just begun. Rain slapped against the asphalt roof-tiles, gurgled down the drainpipe and pattered on the leaves of the overhanging trees. In the background, it hissed as it fell on the lake. Distant flashes of lightning and deep rumblings of thunder warned of the coming storm.

Happy with his solitude and his cleverness, Quilley linked his hands behind his head and leaned back in the chair. Out back, he heard the rustling of a small animal making its way through the undergrowth -- a raccoon, perhaps, or even a skunk. When he closed his eyes, he pictured all the trees, shrubs and wild flowers around the cottage and marvelled at what deadly potential so many of them contained.

* * * * * * *

The sun blazed down on the back patio of the Madison, a small garden protected from the wind by high fences. Quilley wore his sunglasses and nursed a pint of Conners Ale. The place was packed. Skilled and pretty waitresses came and went, trays laden with baskets of chicken wings and golden pints.

The two of them sat out of the way at a white table in a corner by the metal fire escape. A striped parasol offered some protection, but the sun was still too hot and bright. Peplow's wife must have given him hell about drinking the last time, because today he had ordered only a Coke.

"It was easy," Quilley said. "You could have done it yourself. The only setback was that foxgloves don't grow wild here like they do in England. But you're gardener; you grow them."

Peplow shook his head and smiled. "It's the gift of clever people like yourself to make difficult things seem easy. I'm not particularly resourceful, Mr Quilley. Believe me, I wouldn't have known where to start. I had no idea that such a book existed, but you did, because of your art. Even if I had known, I'd hardly have dared buy it or take it out of the library for fear that someone would remember. But you've had your copy for years. A simple tool of the trade. No, Mr Quilley, please don't underestimate your contribution. I was a desperate man. Now you've given me a chance at freedom. If there's anything at all I can do for you, please don't hesitate to say. I'd consider it an honour."

"This collection of yours," Quilley said. "What does it consist of?"

"British and Canadian crime fiction, mostly. I don't like to boast, but it's a very good collection. Try me. Go on, just mention a name."

"E.C.R. Lorac."

"About twenty of the Inspector MacDonalds. First editions, mint condition."

"Anne Hocking?"

"Everything but *Night's Candles.*"

"Trotton?"

Peplow raised his eyebrows. "Good Lord, that's an obscure one. Do you know, you're the first person I've come across who's ever mentioned that."

"Do you have it?"

"Oh, yes." Peplow smiled smugly. "X.J. Trotton, *Summer's Lease*, published 1942. It turned up in a pile of junk I bought at an auction some years ago. It's rare, but not very valuable. Came out in Britain during the war and probably died an immediate death. It was his only book, as far as I can make out, and there is no biographical information. Perhaps it was a pseudonym for someone famous?"

Quilley shook his head. "I'm afraid I don't know. Have you read it?"

"Good Lord, no! I don't read them. It could damage the spines. Many of them are fragile. Anything I want to read -- like your books -- I buy in paperback."

"Mr Peplow," Quilley said slowly, "you asked if there was anything you could do for me. As a matter of fact, there *is* something you can give me for my services."

"Yes?"

"The Trotton."

Peplow frowned and pursed his thin lips. "Why on earth...?"

"For my own collection, of course. I'm especially interested in the war period."

Peplow smiled. "Ah! So that's how you knew so much about them? I'd no idea you were a collector, too."

Quilley shrugged modestly. He could see Peplow struggling, visualizing the gap in his collection. But finally the poor man decided that the murder of his wife was more important to him than an obscure mystery novel. "Very well," he said gravely. "I'll mail it to you."

"How can I be sure...?"

Peplow looked offended. "I'm a man of my word, Mr Quilley. A bargain is a bargain." He held out his hand. "Gentleman's agreement."

"All right." Quilley believed him. "You'll be in touch, when it's done?"

"Yes. Perhaps a brief note in with the Trotton, if you can wait that long. Say two or three weeks?"

"Fine. I'm in no hurry."

Quilley hadn't examined his motives since the first meeting, but he had realized, as he passed on the information and instructions, that it was the challenge he responded to more than anything else. For years he had been writing crime novels, and in providing Peplow with the means to kill his slatternly, overbearing wife, Quilley had derived some vicarious pleasure from the knowledge that he -- Inspector Baldry's creator -- could bring off in real life what he had always been praised for doing in fiction.

Quilley also knew that there were no real detectives who possessed Baldry's curious mixture of intellect and instinct. Most of them were thick plodders, and they would never realize that dull Mr Peplow had murdered his wife with a bunch of foxgloves, of all things. Nor would they ever know that the brains behind the whole affair had been none other than his, Dennis Quilley's.

The two men drained their glasses and left together. The corner of Bloor and Spadina was busy with tourists and students lining up for charcoal-grilled hot-dogs from the street-vendor. Peplow turned towards the subway and Quilley wandered among the artsy crowd and sidewalk cyclists on Bloor Street West for a while, then he settled at an open air cafe over a daiquiri and a slice of kiwi-fruit cheesecake to read the *Globe and Mail.*

Now, he thought as he sipped his drink and turned to the arts section, all he had to do was wait. One day soon, a small package would arrive for him. Peplow would be free of his wife, and Quilley would be the proud owner of one of the few remaining copies of X.J. Trotton's one and only mystery novel, *Summer's Lease.*

*   *   *   *   *

Three weeks passed, and no package arrived. Occasionally, Quilley thought of Mr Peplow and wondered what had become of him. Perhaps he had lost his nerve after all. That wouldn't be surprising. Quilley knew that he would have no way of finding out what had happened if Peplow chose not to contact him again. He didn't know where the man lived or where he worked. He didn't even know if Peplow was his real name. Still, he thought, it was best that way. No contact. Even the Trotton wasn't worth being involved in a botched murder for.

Then, at ten o'clock one warm Tuesday morning in September, the doorbell chimed. Quilley looked at his watch and frowned. Too early for the postman. Sighing, he pressed the SAVE command on his PC and walked down to answer the door. A stranger stood there, an overweight woman in a yellow polka-dot dress with short sleeves and a low neck. She had piggy eyes set in a round face, and dyed red hair that looked limp and lifeless after a cheap perm. She carried an imitation crocodile-skin handbag.

Quilley must have stood there looking puzzled for too long. The woman's eyes narrowed and her rosebud mouth tightened so much that white furrows radiated from the red circle of her lips.

"May I come in?" she asked.

Stunned, Quilley stood back and let her enter. She walked straight over to a wicker armchair and sat down. The basket-work creaked under her. From there, she surveyed the room, with its waxed parquet floor, stone fireplace and antique Ontario furniture.

"Nice," she said, clutching her purse on her lap. Quilley sat down opposite her. Her dress was a size too small and the material strained over her red. fleshy upper arms and pinkish bosom. The hem rode up as she crossed her legs, exposing a wedge of fat, mottled thigh. Primly, she pulled it down again over her dimpled knees.

"I'm sorry to appear rude," said Quilley, regaining his composure, "but who the hell are you?"

"My name is Peplow," the woman said. "Mrs Gloria Peplow. I'm a widow."

Quilley felt a tingling sensation along his spine, like he always did when fear began to take hold of him.

He frowned and said, "I'm afraid I don't know you, do I?"

"We've never met," the woman replied, "but I think you knew my husband."

"I don't recall any Peplow. Perhaps you're mistaken?"

Gloria Peplow shook her head and fixed him with her piggy eyes. He noticed they were black, or as near as. "I'm not mistaken, Mr Quilley. You didn't only know my husband, you also plotted with him to murder me."

Quilley flushed and jumped to his feet. "That's absurd! Look, if you've come here to make insane accusations like that, you'd better go." He stood like an ancient statue, one hand pointing dramatically towards the door.

Mrs Peplow smirked. "Oh, sit down. You look very foolish standing there like that."

Quilley continued to stand. "This is *my* home, Mrs Peplow, and I insist that you leave. Now!"

Mrs Peplow sighed and opened the gilded plastic clasp on her purse. She took out a Shoppers Drug Mart envelope, picked out two colour photographs, and dropped them next to the Wedgewood dish on the antique wine table by her chair. Leaning forward, Quilley could see clearly what they were: one showed him standing with Peplow outside the Park Plaza, and the other caught the two of them talking outside the Scotiabank at Bloor and Spadina. Mrs Peplow flipped the photos over, and Quilley saw that they had been date-stamped by the processors.

"You met with my husband at least twice to help him plan my death."

"That's ridiculous. I do remember him, now I've seen the picture. I just couldn't recollect his name. He was a fan. We talked about mystery novels. I'm very sorry to hear that he's passed away."

"He had a heart attack, Mr Quilley, and now I'm all alone in the world."

"I'm very sorry, but I don't see...."

Mrs Peplow waved his protests aside. Quilley noticed the dark sweat stain on the tight material around her armpit. She fumbled with the catch on her purse again and brought out a pack of Export Lights and a book of matches.

"I don't allow smoking in my house," Quilley said. "It doesn't agree with me."

"Pity," she said, lighting the cigarette and dropping the spent match in the Wedgewood bowl. She blew a stream of smoke directly at Quilley, who coughed and fanned it away.

"Listen to me, Mr Quilley," she said, "and listen good. My husband might have been stupid, but I'm not. He was not only a pathetic and boring little man, he was also an open book. Don't ask me why I married him. He wasn't even much of a man, if you know what I mean. Do you think I haven't known for some time that he was thinking of ways to get rid of me? I wouldn't give him a divorce because the one thing he did -- the *only* thing he did -- was provide for me, and he didn't even do that very well. I'd have got half if we divorced, but half of what he earned isn't enough to keep a bag-lady. I'd have had to go to work, and I don't like that idea. So I watched him. He got more and more desperate, more and more secretive. When he started looking smug, I knew he was up to something."

"Mrs Peplow," Quilley interrupted, "this is all very well, but I don't see what it has to do with me. You come in here and pollute my home with smoke, then you start telling me some fairy tale about your husband, a man I met casually once or twice. I'm busy, Mrs Peplow, and quite frankly I'd rather you left and let me get back to work."

"I'm sure you would." She flicked a column of ash into the Wedgewood bowl. "As I was saying, I knew he was up to something, so I started following him. I thought he might have another woman, unlikely as it seemed, so I took my camera along. I wasn't really surprised when he headed for the Park Plaza instead of going back to the office after lunch one day. I watched the elevator go up to the nineteenth floor, the bar, so I waited across the street in the crowd for him to come out again. As you know, I didn't have to wait very long. He came out with you. And it was just as easy the next time."

"I've already told you, Mrs Peplow," he was a mystery buff, a fellow collector, that's all --

"Yes, yes, I know he was. Him and his stupid catalogues and collection. Still," she mused, "it had its uses. That's how I found out who you were. I'd seen your picture on the book covers, of course. If I may say so, it does you more than justice." She looked him up and down as if he were a side of beef hanging in a butcher's window. He cringed. "As I was saying, my husband was obvious. I knew he must be chasing you for advice. He spends so much time escaping to his garden or his little world of books that it was perfectly natural he would go to a mystery novelist for advice rather than to a real criminal. I imagine you were a bit more accessible, too. A little flattery, and you were hooked. Just another puzzle for you to work on."

"Look, Mrs Peplow --"

"Let me finish." She ground out her cigarette butt in the bowl. "Foxgloves, indeed! Do you think he could manage to brew up a dose of digitalis without leaving traces all over the place? Do you know what he did the first time? He put just enough in my Big Mac to make me a bit nauseous and make my pulse race, but he left the leaves and stems in the dustbin! Can you believe that? Oh, I became very careful in my eating habits after that, Mr Quilley. Anyway, your little plan didn't work. I'm here and he's dead."

Quilley paled. "My God, you killed him, didn't you?"

"He was the one with the bad heart, not me." She lit another cigarette.

"You can hardly blackmail me for plotting with your husband to kill you when *he's* the one who's dead," said Quilley. "And as for evidence, there's nothing. No, Mrs Peplow, I think you'd better go, and think yourself lucky I don't call the police."

Mrs Peplow looked surprised. "What are you talking about? I have no intention of blackmailing you for plotting to kill me."

"Then what...?"

"Mr Quilley, my husband was blackmailing you. That's why *you* killed *him*."

Quilley slumped back in his chair. "I what?"

She took a sheet of paper from her purse and passed it over to him. On it were just two words: "Trotton -- Quilley". He recognized the neat handwriting. "That's a photocopy," Mrs Peplow went on. "The original's where I found it, slipped between the pages of a book called *Summer's Lease* by X.J. Trotton. Do you know that book, Mr Quilley?"

"Vaguely. I've heard of it."

"Oh, have you? It might also interest you to know that along with that book and the slip of paper, locked away in my husband's files, is a copy of your own first novel. I put it there."

Quilley felt the room spinning around him. "I...I...." Peplow had given him the impression that Gloria was stupid, but that was turning out to be far from the truth.

"My husband's only been dead for two days. If the doctors look, they'll *know* that he's been poisoned. For a start, they'll find high levels of potassium, and then they'll discover eosinophilia. Do you know what they are, Mr Quilley? I looked them up. They're a kind of white blood cell, and you find lots of them around if there's been any allergic reaction or inflammation. If I was to go to the police and say I'd been suspicious about my husband's behaviour over the past few weeks, that I had followed him and photographed him with you, and if they were to find the two books and the slip of paper in his files....Well, I think you know what they'd make of it, don't you? Especially if I told them he came home feeling ill after a lunch with you."

"It's not fair," Quilley said, banging his fist on the chair arm. "It's just not bloody fair."

"Life rarely is. But the police aren't to know how stupid and unimaginative my husband was. They'll just look at the note, read the books, and assume he was blackmailing you." She laughed. "Even if Frank had read the Trotton book, I'm sure he'd have only noticed an 'influence,' at the most. But you and I know what really went on, don't we? It happens more often than people think. Only recently I was reading in the newspaper about similarities between a book by Colleen McCullough and *The Blue Castle* by Lucy Maud Montgomery. I'd say that was a bit obvious, wouldn't you? It was much easier in your case, much less dangerous. You were very clever, Mr Quilley. You found an obscure novel, and you didn't only adapt the plot for your own first book, you even stole the character of your series detective. There was some risk involved, certainly, but not much. Your book is better, without a doubt. You have some writing talent, which X.J. Trotton completely lacked. But he did have the germ of an original idea, and it wasn't lost on you, was it?"

Quilley groaned. Thirteen solid police procedurals, twelve of them all his own work, but the first, yes, a deliberate adaptation of a piece of ephemeral trash. He had seen what Trotton could have done and had done it himself. Serendipity, or so it had seemed when he found the dusty volume in a second-hand bookshop in Victoria years ago. All he had had to do was change the setting from London to Toronto, alter the names, and set about improving upon the original. And now...? The hell of it was that he would have been perfectly safe without the damn book. He had simply given in to the urge to get his hands on Peplow's copy and destroy it. It wouldn't have mattered, really. *Summer's Lease* would have remained unread on Peplow's shelf. If only the bloody fool hadn't written that note....

"Even if the police can't make a murder charge stick," Mrs Peplow went on, "I think your reputation would suffer if this got out. Oh, the great reading public might not care. Perhaps a trial would even increase your sales -- you know how ghoulish people are -- but the plagiarism would at the very least lose you the respect of your peers. I don't think your agent and publisher would be very happy, either. Am I making myself clear?"

Pale and sweating, Quilley nodded. "How much?" he whispered.

"Pardon?"

"I said how much. How much do you want to keep quiet?"

"Oh, it's not your money I'm after, Mr Quilley, or may I call you Dennis? Well, not *only* money, anyway. I'm a widow now. I'm all alone in the world."

She looked around the room, her piggy eyes glittering, then gave Quilley one of the most disgusting looks he'd ever had in his life.

"I've always fancied living near the lake," she said, reaching for another cigarette. "Live here alone, do you?"

Jack Barnao

Jack Barnao is a Canadian writer who flew with
the RAF. His popular thrillers, *HannerLocke*
and *Locke-Step*, feature Canadian born, SAS
trained bodyguard John Locke. Barnao is also an
avid fisherman and outdoorsman. Both loves
shine through in the following story, his only
published short fiction, in which two anglers
after bass end up finding bigger fish to fry.

THAT WAS NO LADY

by Jack Barnao

Around four in the afternoon the wind dropped and the bass started hitting. Chuck got a ouple of breakfast-sized fish on his bucktail Mepps and then a solid one took my Flatfish under the canoe. I sat there, swivelling in the seat to follow the wonderful electric surgings as he dived for the logs then changed his plans and walked on the water on his tail until at last he tired himself out and Chuck netted him. We toasted him with a can of beer each, then set off to paddle up the lake to the lodge.

We slid back over the flat black water between pink basalt rocks and the birches and conifers of Ontario cottage country. Not that there are any cottages on this lake. Apparently it once belonged holus-bolus to a railroad tycoon. His original cabin is the three storey lodge in which Chuck and I were staying for the week. So far we hadn't seen any other buildings on the lake but there was one, according to the lodge owner. He's been there since the end of the Second War and he knows everything about everybody. "The owner of this place had a brother, he built a cottage, well, quite a house, you'd call it in today's terms, that would have been around 1920," he told us. "You'll see it if you paddle up the West Arm."

And now we saw it, pretentious by modern standards, a big frame place in need of painting. It had a verandah around the whole downstairs and a balcony upstairs along the front which naturally overlooked the lake. From thirty yards out it had a kind of magic to it, filling me with a nostalgia for some place or time I'd never known. I could imagine the original owners sitting on the verandah in the summer, eating home-made ice cream and talking about history as it was happening.

And then I saw the girl. She was standing inside the French door that opened on to the upstairs balcony. She was blonde and slim and, most startling of all, she seemed to be naked.

I guess the sight made me miss the water with my paddle and Chuck corrected and glanced back. "Stay tuned, Cy," he told me. "We've still got a mile to go."

Looking back over his big shoulder he caught sight of the way I was staring and followed my gaze. "Looking at the old guy on the deck there?" he wondered.

I know how voices carry over the water so I said, "Yeah, let's go show him the fish. Neighbourly thing to do." I could see the old man now, sitting on an honest-to-god rocking chair almost directly beneath the girl who had come all the way out of the window now and was standing at the rail of the balcony, the blonde pubic puff showing golden below the unpainted wood of the top rail.

Chuck said, "Holy Moly", and dug into the water awkwardly, as I had done when I saw her. He turned to grin at me. "Now I know what put you off your stroke," he said.

I laughed and we paddled across, moving slowly so we wouldn't reach the dock too quickly and let the man on the verandah realize we were gazing up over his head. And meanwhile the girl on the balcony was laughing silently, rocking back with one hand over her mouth, the other on the rail, her sweet young breasts firm and round against the taut flesh over her rib cage, every muscle in her long legs delineated. "This is better'n Playboy," Chuck growled at me over his shoulder.

Finally the old man saw we were coming in. He got up from the rocker and walked down to the rotting old dock to greet us. He paused as soon as he had left the verandah to look upwards, nervously, at the balcony and in the instant in which my eyes followed his movement, the girl had vanished.

We were too close to him for any comment or even to glance up at the balcony without making it obvious so I concentrated on beaming at him and grabbing the dock. He was perhaps seventy-five, lean and hollow-faced, in that eroded way that slim men develop in old age. His hair was cut in a brush and was white as paper. He looked down at us without speaking.

Chuck said, "How're you today?"

He nodded once or twice, then spoke. "Just fine. Yourselves?"

"Good," Chuck said heartily. He has the beefy self-confidence of the long time copper. You couldn't dislike him unless you were some kind of political activist. He's totally disarming. "Thought we'd show you the fish," he said, and pulled up the stringer we'd filled. Most of them were smallish, only mine was worth comment. The old man looked down at them thoughtfully as if he was going to be asked to judge them for some contest. "I've caught a whole string of bass that size, plenny o' times," he said, without pride, pointing at my biggest one.

"Yeah, well, we've all had days like that," Chuck said. I had taken the opportunity to glance up at the balcony and I saw the girl again. She was inside the French door, still naked, posing for us now, holding her long blonde hair up with one hand, caressing her breast with the other. It was devastating and I had to look down at the fish and try not to think about her for a minute before I could join in the conversation that Chuck had prodded into being.

"Used to be better," the old man was saying. "Used to be that a man could catch his dinner inside half an hour, any time of day or night, right off the dock here. Place is fished almost out now."

"Why's that then?" Chuck asked innocently. He had dropped his baseball cap in the bottom of the canoe and was looking up at the old man, artfully shading his eyes with his hand. I could tell that he was looking up and beyond at that irresistible blonde in the upper doorway. I copied him and saw her again, her mouth half open in laughter at our embarrassment. This time I stared at her, I couldn't help myself. She was young and fresh, not beautiful in her face, her nose was too snub and her eyes might have been set a little further apart for real beauty but she wore no makeup and there was a sexual exuberance to her that I have never seen in any of the meet-market singles bars in Toronto. This was a live one. And I wondered what the Hell she was doing hanging around this old goat who was certainly qualified to be her grandfather.

"Over-fishing," the old man was saying, sadly. "I guess it would be fairer to say overpopulation, that's the truth but nobody wants to hear it. I blame those people in Ottawa, they'll let anybody into the country."

Chuck started to pump, the way a seasoned investigator will, moving in obliquely to find out the facts. "You up here for the whole summer?" he asked.

The old man snorted. "Year round," he said. "It's peaceful but it gets a little lonesome sometimes."

"Lonesome?" I asked innocently and he swung his eyes to me sharply like a frail old hawk.

"You saw her, didn't you?" he demanded.

Chuck took over without a flicker, as a cop he's better in this kind of courtroom situation than I will ever be. "Saw who?"

The old man looked at him, hard-eyed, then at me, then spat. "The blonde girl." He hooked his thumb over his shoulder at the balcony and we both glanced up but there was no sign of the girl. We both looked back at him, smiling in a puzzled way like you might do to a child who's asked some impossible question.

"Don't go grinning at me," he said sharply. "Blonde, kind of slim, likely naked as a jaybird, flaunting her body so that every young buck who passes feels his sap rising and paddles over to see if he can take advantage of her." He spat again, in fury. "That don't take any great ability, you know. You don't have to be smart or handsome or rich, even."

Chuck held up one hand, "Now don't get fired up. What you think about anything is your own business. We dropped in to be sociable, if you want us to leave, just say so."

The old man looked at him for as long as it takes to draw a couple of slow breaths. Then he began to smile himself, but only with his mouth, his eyes were hard as stones. "You think I'm just a jealous old goat with a young girl I can't satisfy, don't you?"

We said nothing and he rapped out the question again. "Don't you?"

"I don't think anything of the kind, but it's a free country, you suit yourself what you think," I said carefully. It seemed certain he was crazy. Maybe the girl was as well. Maybe she was his nymphomaniac daughter or granddaughter and he hid her up here where she couldn't get into the kind of trouble that's waiting behind every door in the city.

He looked at me now, concentrating, staring almost through me with those hard old eyes. "I'm going to tell you something you won't believe," he said at last.

"Listen, you don't have to tell us anything. We're just passing by." Chuck had formed the same opinion as me, I judged. He wanted the old man cooled out before we left so he wouldn't run for his deer rifle and put a couple of slugs into us as we paddled away. The old man ignored him. He must have decided that I was the leader.

"There is no girl," he said and then laughed, a nasty squeaky laugh like fingernails on a blackboard. "You're not going to sleep with her, or even get your hands on her. She doesn't exist."

Chuck turned to me. "I figure we should be heading back," he began but the old man interrupted him.

"She's a ghost," he said triumphantly. "She died years ago. Right here, fell off that balcony and broke her neck. Only she won't go away and leave me alone. She keeps doing this, bringing men over here, tormenting me, even though she's dead."

"Get serious," Chuck said. He turned to me again. "I've heard enough of this hogwash. Let's go."

"No." The old man was frantic. He laid a cold hand on my shoulder and in spite of the July heat and the effort I'd spent in paddling the canoe, it seemed to frost me right through to my bones. "Please," he said, frantically. "Please take a minute to check upstairs. I'll go with you."

I looked at Chuck and he was grinning again. I could see he was thinking, Why not? Maybe the blonde will be sitting up there and we can get a little better acquainted, maybe she will even ask us to take her away from this old fruitcake. That wouldn't be unpleasant.

"If it won't take more'n a minute," he said and the old man laughed out loud.

"Come on. Come on," he called over his shoulder as he led the way up to the cottage. Chuck and I exchanged glances, then he grinned and I shrugged and we followed. Chuck went first and the old verandah groaned under his weight. I glanced around as we crossed it. There were two wicker chairs and a low wicker table with a bottle of Gilbey's Lemon Gin on it and a magazine. I saw the date, September 1939. Then the old man and Chuck were inside and I followed them through the old, damp-smelling living room and up a flight of wooden stairs that squealed dangerously under our weight.

"This place could stand a little repair work," Chuck laughed and I echoed a silent Amen. And then we both stood and gaped in amazement. The whole upper storey, two big bedrooms that opened off the landing at the head of the stairs, was empty. The plaster on the walls had fallen out in half a dozen places. The floors were gappy and looked rotten. The windows at the back of the house were all broken.

"There." The old man waved his hand around him like a real estate man showing a bargain. "There, where's the girl now?" He cackled again and I felt the hair rising on the back of my neck.

Chuck wasn't as quick to react. As a policeman he never believes anything without asking some questions. "So, OK, let's say we did see a girl up here. What was to stop her slipping down the stairs and out the back door while we were on the dock?" It made sense to me and I was glad he had asked it but the old man ignored the question completely. "Come on, come and look at the balcony." He led the way over the unsafe-looking floor, moving lightly, and Chuck walked after him, watching every step, making sure to step on the beams beneath the softened old boards with the gaps all around them.

I didn't follow. The tension in that cottage was so great that I couldn't even bear to look down the staircase, in case the blonde girl was standing there, beckoning to me, luring me to follow her down to the gates of Hell.

Chuck whistled from the doorway. "Sonofagun." He turned and frowned at me. "This whole balcony's rotted out. A bird couldn't land out here safely."

"Let's go." I waved him over and he checked me with his calm, policeman's eyes and nodded.

"Yeah, I think that's the right idea." He stepped carefully back beside me, the old man following him, sober-faced now.

"There. You believe me now? You guys have seen a ghost, a real live ... well a real dead ghost."

"Come on," Chuck told him, like a cop on a crossing calling a child across the intersection. "Let's get outside and talk about this some more."

We went downstairs, me first, looking anxiously around, every nerve in my body ablaze with tension, expecting at every step to see the blonde woman gliding towards me, long hair floating about her like smoke from the fires of Hell. I shuddered convulsively and Chuck said, "Relax, Cy, there was nothing there."

"Just because there was nothing you could shoot doesn't mean there was nothing there," I told him. "I'm not a copper, I don't have to be convinced about everything like you do. I've seen enough."

I didn't stop moving until we were out by the canoe again, all three of us. The old man looked at us both and held up his hands, helplessly. "Now you know what I live with," he said gently. "She's been dead for years but she won't leave me alone. What am I going to do?"

"If it was me I'd burn this place down and get myself back to the city where there were some people around," Chuck said grimly and I could see that his tough cop shell hadn't saved him from the horror I felt.

"Yes, that's a good idea," I agreed. "Anyway, good luck. Why not come up to the lodge later on, have a drink with us."

"I'd like that," the old man said wistfully. "I'd like that very much."

He said nothing more as we cast off, waved to him and paddled out under the weight of the late afternoon sun. I glanced back once and saw him standing where we had left him, one hand over his eyes as he followed our passage down the lake.

I tried to talk about the girl as we docked the canoe at the lodge but Chuck stopped me with one upraised finger. "Not one word," he cautioned. "We think we saw things. Maybe we did see things but if we talk this up, we'll end up in a rubber room with guys looking in at us through a little window."

"But we saw her, clear as day," I protested. "You saw her too, slim, good looking, naked as the day she was born. There was no white sheet, no howling. That was a real girl."

"Yeah. And we've been drinking real beer and yukking it up all day and the only sane decision any headshrinker would come to is that we were drunk," Chuck said. "Drunk or crazy. Take your pick."

So instead of sharing our story, we cleaned our fish and took them around to the kitchen, then headed for the lounge. The owner was sitting at the bar reading a week-old copy of the Toronto Star. We ordered scotches and he asked about the fishing and then Chuck asked, "What do you know about the old guy who built the place down the lake?"

"Quite a story," he said. "He did time for murder, you know that?"

"No fooling," Chuck was a cop, instantly. "Who'd he ice?"

The landlord pulled himself a single shot of J & B and cradled the shot glass in his hand as he settled more comfortably on his stool, the frustrated story-teller, seizing his opportunity. "His wife," he said, and sipped while Chuck and I looked at one another in amazement.

"Was she an older woman, or what?" Chuck prompted cunningly.

Another sip and the landlord said, "No. Not the way I hear it. She was younger than him by quite a bit, young enough to be his daughter, around twenty I'd guess. Blonde, quite a dish by all accounts. Anyway, rumour has it that she had the roundest heels in the district. He couldn't turn his back on her for a minute. Didn't matter to her who it was, his lawyer was involved, I remember hearing, then the engineer on the private train that used to bring them up here. And then, one night, he's sitting on the verandah downstairs and he hears this noise up above. This is kind of late, the way I hear it, and she's already up in bed. So anyway he incy-winces his way up the stairs without making a sound and there she is in bed with the guy who delivered the ice, some handyman from this place, guy who worked for his brother."

"And then what?" I asked. My flesh was tingling on my neck. Young, blonde, sexual, this was the woman I had seen, the tempt-ress on the balcony.

The landlord sipped noisily, draining his shot glass. He sat with the empty glass in his fingers until Chuck got up and poured him another shot, not speaking, just placing the charged glass back in his hand. He sipped again, narrowing his eyes slightly in appreciation. "The handyman ran for it, just took a run and dived off the verandah into the deep water. Remember this was in the twenties, there was no power boat waiting at the dock to run him down, he was free to swim off on his own, and get back to his boat, or walk around the shore to this place."

"And the wife?" I could see that long, cool hair, with her hand artfully cocked under it, her lithe body, her laughing mouth.

"They say he threw her off the balcony. He said she jumped. In any case, they gave him the benefit of the doubt, they didn't hang him, which was unusual in those days. He went to jail for fifteen years instead."

"Poor bastard," Chuck said. "A wife like that must've been Hell on wheels to live with."

"That's what I hear," the lodge owner said. "And there's more to it than that. She haunted him after he got out. That was the local story anyway. He didn't get rid of her at all. She hung around that place forever. All kinds of people say they've seen her."

Chuck and I looked at one another but neither of us said anything. The owner sniffed and sipped his drink. "Never saw her myself of course but she's supposed to be a real vamp."

I shook my head, sadly. "Imagine being haunted by the worst thing, the thing you hated most about a woman you'd killed. You'd never get any peace at all."

"Poor guy," Chuck said. "You'd get to the point where you'd long to be dead yourself so you could get away from her, or at least deal with her on equal terms. I wonder how he stays sane."

The lodge owner looked at him, frowning slightly. "How do you mean, stays sane? He didn't even last five years. He hanged himself, the same month I joined the service, September, it was, nineteen thirty-nine."

Peter Sellers

Current Chairman of the Crime Writers of Canada,
Peter Sellers is the editor of an earlier Canadian
crime fiction anthology, *COLD BLOOD:
Murder in Canada.* His short stories have appeared in *Mike Shayne Mystery Magazine* and
Detective Story Magazine and twice been listed
on the Honour Roll in the *Year's Best Mystery
and Suspense Stories.* He lives in Toronto, where
he's Associate Creative Director at a prominent
advertising agency.

SOMEWHERE THEY CAN'T FIND ME

by Peter Sellers

They came for Tully early Sunday morning. By the time the door of his cell clanged open he was already dressed and sitting on the edge of his bunk.

"Out, Tully," one of the guards said. There were two of them, both with riot sticks in their hands.

Tully got up and shuffled towards the door. His shoes without laces flopped up and down and chafed his heels but he didn't mind much. He didn't expect a long walk and in his future he saw sandals on his feet and felt sand between his toes. Tully's cellmate, a jailhouse veteran named Larue, poked his head out from under his stiff blanket. His hair stuck out like fur on a wet cat. Which was also how he smelled. "Where you goin', Tully?" he asked with a laugh. "Church?"

Tully grinned back at him. "You could say I'm gonna talk to my saviour."

The guard stepped back and to the side and Tully walked out past him. The guard slammed the cell door shut and locked it and prodded Tully forward with the end of his riot stick.

Larue shook his head and pulled it back under the blanket.

The holding area consisted of a bank of eight cells, each designed to sleep up to four men but at times filled with twice that many. Each cell was locked up separately for the night, then in the morning all the doors opened and the prisoners spilled out into a bullpen about sixteen feet across which ran the length of the eight cell fronts and had a single barred door at one end.

Tully's cell was furthest from the door. They walked the length of the bullpen past eyes which peered out at them without curiosity. The first guard opened the door in front of Tully, they all went through, and the second guard locked it behind them. Tully hoped to God it was the last time he ever heard that noise.

They took Tully to one of the private consultation rooms where prisoners and lawyers got together to work out their plea bargains. This was separate from the regular visiting area which was a big open space watched by armed guards and which visitors where searched on their way into, and prisoners on the way out. The private rooms were not much different from the cells. They were a little bigger and they had tile on the floor, cracked and stained though it was. And there were fans on the ceiling, but they spun around without doing much to improve the air. The big difference was the presence of a small scarred table and a few moulded plastic chairs. After three weeks of nothing to sit on but a board hard bunk or the concrete floor these chairs looked as inviting to Tully as wing chairs in a five star hotel lobby.

There were three men in the room waiting for him. Two of them were the kind of big, hard-eyed men the federal cops have mass produced in a factory somewhere. They stood with their backs to different walls, at right angles to one another, so they wouldn't get caught in a crossfire. They both had the haircuts which the government bought wholesale by the truckload the day after they went out of style. And beneath their jackets they had guns which Tully knew they didn't just fire weekends at the shooting gallery.

The third man was sitting down, legs crossed at the knees. There was a manilla file folder on the table beside him with Tully's name on it. He was holding a cigarette between yellowed fingers. The smoke from it drifted up above his head four or five feet and hung there like a tiny cloud. Although Tully figured it wouldn't have the guts to rain.

"You can go," the man said to the jailhouse guards and they left without a word. He looked at Tully for a long time. Tully returned the favour. "Sit down," he said finally. His voice was flat and nasal. "My name's Loncraine."

Tully smiled. "Oh yeah. Aldo told me about you."

"So you know why I'm here."

"You wanna make a deal."

Loncraine's light brown hair was fashionably longer than the other two cops and his mustache was cut precisely. Tully got the impression he measured and trimmed one hair at a time. He wore an Italian suit and a silk tie and his initials were embroidered on the French cuffs of his shirt. He dropped his cigarette to the floor and ground it out with sharp, rough motions. Then he took another from a silver case and lit it with an old-fashioned flint lighter. "Yes," he said at last. "We're going to make a deal."

"You sound pretty sure of yourself."

"Let's just say I'm pretty sure of you. For one thing, you don't have a lawyer. I know the court appointed one for you and I know he told you about us and I know you had him taken off your case."

Tully laughed. "I didn't need no Legal Aid type," he said, scratching his unshaven jaw. His beard had always come in slowly and after three weeks without a razor it was at that irritated stage that had always made him shave it off before. He thought he might leave it on this time, though. It fit, somehow, with his new image of himself. "They're fine if you got the need or you don't got the dough.

These are not my problems. It ain't the money, it's the principle. Me, I'm a principled guy. Some people might think 'Who the hell is he trying to kid?' but it's true. I never cut nobody wasn't trying to cut me. I never stuck a gun in nobody's ribs that wasn't trying to stick one in mine first. And I never lied to nobody. I may have run for Nick and Tony and the mob but my word is my bond, okay? And when I started with 'em they told me, 'Tully, you ever get busted all you gotta do is call and we'll take care of you.' Lawyer, bail and everything. So I get busted and the court gives me this Legal Aid guy. I gave him the brush and I called like they said. Three weeks later I'm still sitting on my ass and I ain't heard one lousy word of Latin yet."

Loncraine listened without expression or movement. The ash grew on the motionless cigarette until it fell to the floor of its own weight. When Tully had finished he said, "That's how I know we're going to make a deal."

"Just like Renzo did?"

Loncraine nodded. "He told me the same story, Tully."

Renzo had been gathered up, like Tully, in one of the federal government's periodic sweeps of organized crime. He'd parlayed his inside knowledge and his relative unimportance into a position as a star Crown Witness and the promise of a new life under the Witness Relocation Program. Three days before he took the stand, he called Tully to say good-bye and to mention Loncraine, should Tully ever want out himself.

"Right now, Tully, Nick and Tony and everybody else we picked up, all of whom have posted extremely large bonds for themselves by the way, are only thinking about their own necks. They don't give a damn about you. Never did. You're going to take a fall for them and they're going to rely on your loyalty and fear to keep you quiet. And yes, we could very easily put you away. Which, principled or not, is where you belong. But we're not going to do that because, Tully, you're nothing. You're a piece of filler on page thirty. Those other guys are headlines. And we're after headlines."

"You really know how to make a guy feel wanted."

Loncraine laughed. "Don't worry. After word gets out of what you're going to do, they'll make you feel very wanted."

Tully tried not to shudder. "I go along, you get your headlines. What do I get?"

"Something more like what Renzo's got."

Tully had this picture of Renzo he just couldn't shake. He saw him lying back in a beach chair on some sun drenched stretch of white Polynesian sand that started at the edge of a turquoise sea and ran straight back past Renzo's chair to a line of distant palm trees waving in the breeze like one-armed cheerleaders. Renzo's face was pink beneath a broad straw hat and his grin was wide and crooked. And all the time dark skinned girls wearing nothing but sarongs and carob oil brought him rum punch and kisses.

Tully said, "Where do I sign?"

After that it was quick.

"You realize, of course, the size of the risk you're taking."

Tully shrugged. "I've been to prison before. But I've never been to Fiji."

"Okay. We'll get you out of here as soon as we can. Then we'll make sure you get safely to the trial and, once the trial is completed and the verdicts are in, we handle your relocation. Then you're on your own. Any questions?"

"Two. First, after this is over, I'd like to thank Renzo for giving me your name."

Loncraine shook his head. "No, Tully. We don't release any information about people in our program to anyone. We wouldn't tell Renzo's mother where he is. What's the second question?"

"I was just hoping you'd move me oughta here right away." Tully hoped his nervousness didn't show.

Loncraine shook his head again. "You'll be fine for the time being. It won't be long." He pointed at one of the cops, who had been standing silently the whole time. The cop slipped from the room and returned with Tully's guards.

"You guys always do this on Sunday morning?" Tully asked as he stood up.

Loncraine stood too. "We got a trial in less than two weeks. We want to nail these bastards. We don't have time to waste." He shook the wrinkles out of his suit, tucked the file under his arm and left with his two escorts in tow.

Tully went back to his cell. Larue was still in bed. He lifted his head when Tully came back in. "You don't look any less damned than you did before," he said.

Tully stared at him, irritated by the delay and Larue's smirk. "All things come to him who waits," Tully said as the most Biblical thing that came to mind.

"Christ almighty," Larue said and turned to face the wall.

*   *   *   *   *

The next morning it was Larue's turn. They came and told him he had a visitor. This surprised him and he spent a long time sitting on the edge of his bunk scratching his head until the guards got impatient and dragged him from the cell.

Larue had spent seventeen of his thirty-eight years behind bars of one kind or another. Either as a convict or, in one of his few attempts at going straight, as a bartender until he was caught pouring short shots with one hand and shortchanging the till with the other. In all that time, no one had come to visit him except court appointed lawyers and his mother, twice when he was still a juvenile. But after he got out from his second stint he learned that she'd moved and left no forwarding address. The thought of a visitor both puzzled and scared him.

It didn't surprise Tully. He set about making his bed, tucking the corners in loose instead of in the tight military fashion he prefered. He was working at the head when he heard footsteps behind him and a rough voice whispered his name.

Tully spun around ripping the coarse prison issue blanket from the bed and swinging it in front of him. The knife tore into it and Tully pushed the blanket forward and grabbed a thick forearm as it sliced up past his face and twisted it away from him, seeing the blade dimly in the weak light.

The attacker shoved Tully back, knocking him onto the bunk and fighting to pull his arm free. His other hand threw wild punches at Tully's head and gouged at his eyes. Tully tried frantically to squirm to his feet but fell off the bunk and the assassin landed on top of him, pinning Tully to the floor.

Desperately, Tully bent his head forward and sank his teeth into the arm. He tasted salt and sweat and sank his teeth deeper until he felt the hot spurt of blood which gagged him. He drew back, choking and spitting, and only then did he hear the screams. The knife lay on the floor beside him and the arm was yanked away. Tully spun onto his stomach, picked up the knife and turned on his attacker who was doubled over across the cell with his left hand clutching his bitten arm. Tully jumped on his back and buried the knife in his side, holding onto it like a handle on a mechanical bull as the man bellowed and shook and tried to knock Tully loose by slamming him against the wall. Tully pulled the knife out and plunged it in again and again, each time driving out a cry of higher pitch and greater intensity. By the time he heard footsteps running across the bullpen, the man lay on the floor, the blade sticking from his throat.

Tully looked down at him and recognized him as a con named Baker who'd come in the day before. The knife, he noticed then, was made from the sharpened handle of a spoon.

Two guards, bristling with shotguns, burst into the cell. Tully looked at them angrily. "Put those god damn things away and get me the hell outa here," he said. "I want solitary and I want it now."

As they took him out to one of the jail's three isolation cells, Tully couldn't stop wondering just who the hell Nick had sent to see Larue.

*   *   *   *   *

Tully was only in solitary a few days. Even that was too long. The walls were starting to close in on him so tight he woke up sweating thinking he was in a casket. And he found himself pacing in tight fast circles, his eyes staring hypnotized at the eyelets where the laces should have been. As he made each tiny circuit it was like he was twisting the knot in his stomach tighter and tighter until, when he heard the big key rasp into the keyhole, he jumped a foot in the air and spun around low with his fists bunched tightly at his sides, thumbs tucked in and knuckles pointing out.

The first thing into the cell was a gun barrel and Tully thought, "Jesus, they're everywhere." But when no shots came he knew it wasn't anybody fulfilling a contract. Then a guard came in, unarmed, brushing past the gun barrel. His riot stick swung from his belt. Two men came in behind the guard and suddenly there was no room to turn around. Tully's immediate impulse was to run at them and shove them out, there wasn't enough oxygen for all of them. He felt the terror rise in his body, starting from his knees and racing upward to settle behind his eyes in a kind of seething burning mass. He was sweating and his heart raced and he wanted to scream but didn't. He knew it would use up too much precious air. Instead he glared at the intruders.

Both men with the guard were big federal types. One was a dark man with black hair that lay in thick bands across the backs of his hands and fingers and with a single eyebrow that ran across his forehead above both eyes. Combined with the bald spot at the back of his head and his receding hair-line he made Tully think of a bear that had been prepped for the electric chair. The guy holding the gun was just as tall but thicker and fairhaired with a racoon mask of freckles spread across his face. He grinned. He looked like some kid from a cartoon who'd grown up and taken steroids.

The dark one spoke first. "I'm Walker," he said. He jerked his thumb towards his partner. "This is Levine." The grin spread wider. "We're going to babysit you till the trial's over."

They took Tully out of the cell and the guard locked it behind them, and Tully wondered if he was afraid some agoraphobic might try to break in. They walked along the damp corridor, past other cells and a guard propped up next to a coffee vending machine. Walker had a gun too, now, a semi-automatic pistol of large calibre that Tully didn't want to be anywhere near if he started firing.

In the wide open spaces of the corridor, Tully gulped down the stale air. "Where are we going?" he asked once he'd had his fill.

"The hell outa here," Levine said. "This environment isn't healthy for you."

"Tell me something I don't know. They got a contract out on me?"

Walker looked over at him and his eyes were as emotionless as buttons. "I thought you wanted us to tell you something you didn't know?"

They stopped walking at a steel door which, Tully could see

through the small wired reinforced window, opened onto a small checkpoint and waiting area. On the other side of that was the door to the outside.

Levine's grin was gone. "We're going out now," he said. "Keep your mouth shut. Move fast, but not any faster than us. Don't run. Keep your head down. Hit the outside door and through. Don't look around. There's a limo out there. Tinted windows and the back door will be open. Just climb in and we'll be right with you. Got it?"

Tully swallowed and nodded and the uniformed guard opened the door. They went through it one at a time and crossed the waiting area in a fast moving knot. The guard stayed well behind. Tully was vaguely aware of a blur of faces as they passed. Then they were gone. Tully wasn't even sure how the door ahead of them opened but it did and they were through and Tully dove into the embrace of the waiting limo with Levine and Walker right behind him and the car door shut before Tully realized he hadn't drawn a breath since they left the corridor. He looked up at Levine and saw that he was grinning again.

They took Tully to a mid-town hotel he'd never been in before but he knew was expensive. He figured the feds weren't paying rack rate. Their room was on the fifteenth floor with a view south over the city that would have been spectacular except they kept the blinds closed and wouldn't let Tully go near the windows.

Four days after they arrived someone came to the door who Walker and Levine must have been expecting because when they opened it only one of them had his gun out. It was a uniformed city cop and he came in carrying a dark blue suit and a new shirt, still in the wrapper, and a burgundy tie. There were also new black leather shoes that looked like they'd been spit shined and a pair of black cotton socks and two pairs of underwear. Tully guessed that was in case his nerves got the better of him. And finally there was a new electric razor. Tully figured the beard was going.

The next morning they got up early and told Tully to shower and shave and get dressed.

"You're on," Walker said.

Tully put the clothes on and his body told him how much they cost but that didn't make his stomach feel any better. He was just finishing his half-Windsor when there was a knock on the door and Loncraine came in. "Are you ready?" he asked.

Tully nodded. "Oh, yeah."

"Just don't get rattled. Do everything Walker and Levine tell you. And don't pay any attention to anybody else once the trial starts. I may see you again after it's over."

"You mean if they don't off me."

Loncraine looked at Tully flatly. "Good luck," he said and left. Five minutes later, so did Tully.

The trip to the courthouse was uneventful but Tully couldn't sit still. He was looking all over and his legs were pumping up and down like pistons.

At the courthouse the car rolled to a stop and they were off before it halted dead. Up the stairs and through the big glass doors without incident and then down the long corridor to the main courtroom behind the high oak doors.

They walked the length of the corridor, Tully sandwiched between Walker and Levine. They walked in step, their arms brushing, the syncopated clicking of their footsteps sounding determined and dangerous. But Tully knew it was a lie. Underneath it he was sick with fear. The closer they got to the courtroom the thicker it got with cops. Uniforms with open holsters mingled with plain clothes with microphones in their ears and Uzis under their coats. They were everywhere. Forming a cordon to hold back the curious and scanning constantly on the lookout for anything that might spell trouble.

At first Tully thought it was a lot of fuss for him, but then he realized they were more likely there to protect the defendants than one Crown Witness. It amazed him that a group of men who did the things these guys had done could inspire the forces of law and order to go to such great lengths to ensure due process. If things were reversed, the accused would just be blown away in an alley and that would be the end of it.

While the cops were watching the crowd, Tully was watching the cops. Any one of them could be on the take. Only there to splash his brains on the wall. And anyone could burst out of the crowd like Jack Ruby and gun him down before anyone else could react. If that happened, Tully hoped at least somebody'd take a good picture of it. Each step closer to the courtroom doors didn't relax him, it just made him feel closer to the time they'd take him out. He didn't think for a minute they'd let him get onto the stand without another attempt. So when the doors swung open he expected to see a shotgun levelled at his belly on the other side. Instead there was a bedlam of more cops, lawyers, reporters and Nick and Tony and the other defendants, all of whom glared at Tully with looks that would've killed anybody with a heart condition.

Then the gavel came down and the trial started. Tully sat and fidgeted through it and what happened went past him until they called his name.

In the end, Tully spent four days on the stand, returning each night to the hotel and going through the same agony every morning. But as each day passed and there were no attempts made he felt closer and closer to freedom.

By the time he was through, he'd given a phone book's worth of names and addresses and he'd supplied a list of cause and effect that made the Begats look like an average family with two kids, two cars and a cat.

He climbed off the stand, weary after his last long day, and he left as he had before except this time knowing he wouldn't be forced back. He was on the last leg and he settled in to the hotel to wait it out.

The trial wrapped up in two more weeks. Tully read the headlines and chuckled. He was on his way.

They'd brought him some casual clothes. A pair of jeans and a plaid shirt, a bomber jacket and Kodiak boots, a pair of aviator Ray-Bans and a baseball cap from a farm implement manufacturer. He slipped into them and he felt more free right away. "How soon till we leave?" he asked.

Walker looked at his watch. "Twenty minutes. They're just giving the car a final check."

Tully figured it wasn't for wiper fluid and tire pressure.

While they were waiting, Loncraine came again. He was dressed like he'd stepped off the pages of the kind of catalogue you don't find in backwoods outhouses. "You're off, Tully," he said.

"Yeah, and I can't say I'm sorry to go."

Loncraine nodded. He'd heard that song before. "I just didn't want you to go thinking we don't appreciate all the risks you've taken. And everyone, right up to the Attorney General, is very pleased with the results."

Tully shrugged. "It was a way out."

The phone in the room rang softly. Walker picked up the receiver but said nothing into it before hanging up. "They're ready for us," he told Levine.

"Let's go."

Tully waved at Loncraine and they slipped out the door and down the hall to the waiting service elevator. It rattled its way down much too slowly for Tully who twitched and fidgeted and watched the floor numbers descending like in a nightmare. Finally they shook to a stop and the door opened and Walker and Levine went out first. The car was there waiting and they got inside. Walker climbed behind the wheel, Tully slipped into the passenger seat and Levine sat in the back. By the time the door shut solidly and locked behind them the car was already away from the curb and rolling.

"Where to?" Tully asked, excitement rising in him despite the tension.

"Nowhere special just yet," Walker said.

"Let's just see who's following us," Levine explained.

"If anybody." Walker said it as though he never doubted for a second that someone would.

They threaded through downtown traffic for several blocks, crossing on more than one red so no one could pull up beside them at an intersection.

After half an hour, Tully said, "Jesus it's hot in here."

"It won't kill you," Walker told him.

"Can't we roll down a window or something?"

Levine reached forward and rapped the window beside Tully's head with a knuckle. "Bulletproof," he said.

"Bullet resistant," Walker corrected without taking his eyes off the road.

Tully tugged at his collar. "I'm sweating like a pig."

Levine stared at Tully and Walker stared at the road. "Then shut up," Levine said. "Talking raises the body temperature."

Tully shut up and Levine settled back into the shadows of the back seat.

Ten minutes later, Walker said, "You got 'em?"

"Yeah," Levine said.

"What're you talking about?" Tully asked.

"We're being followed," Levine told him.

"Wine Mustang. Three cars back," Walker added.

"You sure?" Tully asked.

Walker and Levine didn't say anything and Tully pressed his back hard against the seat and he could feel his heart pounding.

The car was heading south now on a stretch of road which wound through a valley beside a brown and sluggish river. At its very bottom it lead into an urban wasteland of unused spur lines and scrap metal yards populated more by idle freight cars and rusting automobiles than people.

"This is perfect for us," Levine said.

"Christ, this is perfect for them," Tully screamed.

"Stay calm," Levine said as he took a shotgun from under the seat and pumped a shell into the chamber.

"Stay down," Walker said.

Tully slipped off the seat and crouched below the level of the padded dash. He looked over at Walker who was driving faster now, but looking almost continually back in the rearview mirror.

"No cars," he said quietly. "Now." And Tully watched as he reached over and lowered the power window to Levine's right. Tully's heart beat even faster.

Then Walker's foot jerked off the gas like it had been burned and it hammered down on the brake and the car shuddered and squealed and skidded as Walker wrenched the wheel around in a hard arc and Tully pitched forward against the dash as the tail of the car swung around wildly and then he was tossed back against the seat again as Walker's foot jumped back on the gas and the car fired forward, rushing towards the oncoming Mustang. Tully couldn't see the other car but he could imagine the confusion. Then the violent roar of the shotgun buried his thoughts. In the confined space the sound hammered its way into his brain and he threw his hands over his ears but each succeeding crash only seemed louder and louder until his head grew numb. Looking back he saw Levine, gun barrel out the open window, firing and pumping and firing and pumping, spent shell casings popping into the air and spinning through the smoke to disappear behind the car. In the brief instants between the firing, Tully heard the whine of car engines and the shattering of glass and once, he thought, the sound of a man screaming. Then, above his head, the window cracked and he looked up to see it flare into a spiderweb pattern but it didn't break. A moment later, Levine drew the gun back inside the car and Walker shut the window again.

"They won't bother us anymore," Levine said.

Tully climbed back up on the seat and looked back to see the Mustang sitting askew in the middle of the road, crippled, smoking and leaking fluids like blood.

Walker reached out to touch the windshield, running a finger along the cracks. "Bulletproof," he said.

As they drove onto a highway which ran west from the city following the line of the lake, Tully started to laugh. "Whatever they're paying you," he said, "it ain't enough."

"We 're just doing our job," Levine said.

They drove further and further into farming country. As they climbed the skyway which took them over to the south side of the lake, Walker asked, "How's it look?"

"All clear," Levine answered.

Tully clapped his hands and rubbed them together. "Sand and sunshine here I come," he chuckled.

Walker laughed. The only time Tully ever heard him do that. "You guys are all the same," he said.

Tully grinned as images of palm trees and native girls danced in his head. Until he felt the cold muzzle of Levine's pistol press against the base of his skull and, in that instant, he realized exactly where Renzo was.

John North

John North was born in England and now practically lives on the golf course. He earns his green fees as a library and systems consultant, mystery reviewer and writer. "Sudden Withdrawal" is his first published fiction, and it owes more to O. Henry than it does to Sam Snead.

SUDDEN WITHDRAWAL

by John North

Alison slowly shifted her weight from one foot to the other as she glanced across the bank to the clock on the far wall. Still only three thirty. With any luck she should be on her way in another forty minutes. She would miss the brightly-painted walls and the dusty rubber plants of the bank, but not the thoughtless customers who looked right through the tellers and most of all, not Ted. Providing her cash balanced, and there were no last-minute snags, she should be in the bus terminal by four thirty with the carefully-packed leather suitcase which she had left in the corner behind the staff room door.

The next customer was a woman in her early fifties whose rouged and powdered face was surmounted by carefully balanced coils of unnaturally black hair. She left the straggling rope-contained line of the late Friday afternoon rush, supporting herself heavily on a black, rubber-tipped walking stick, and slowly approached the wicket. While she waited for her to arrive, Alison wondered again where she had finally found the courage to leave everything behind and walk out on Ted and their marriage. She still had some doubts about the wisdom of her decision and her ability to start over somewhere else, but the uncertainty of the future seemed infinitely preferable to the oppression and futility of the last five years. Her thoughts were interrupted by the hollow thump of a large purse being dropped on her counter. Alison watched as an umbrella, gloves and library books were balanced precariously on the impossibly narrow space which was allocated to the customers.

The woman smiled distractedly but said nothing as she pushed a green slip and some currency across the counter. Preoccupied with her own thoughts she probably did not even notice the pale drawn face and the slightly nervous manner of the petite brown-haired teller who faced her. Alison checked the deposit slip and cash for Amelia Summers' savings account and distractedly brushed her long hair back from her face while she waited for Mary, the teller to her right, to finish a transaction at their shared computer terminal. She began to brood again on her husband's constant state of surly dissatisfaction with her and everything she did. What had happened to turn Ted from the casual happy-go-lucky salesman into the dour worrier she had decided to leave? Not only had she come to dislike him, but it had got so that she didn't particularly like herself. By now she had keyed in the deposit and inserted Mrs. Summers' book.

"Wake up Alison," said the quiet West Indian voice from beside her.

Guiltily, she grabbed the passbook from the machine, and muttered a hasty "Sorry" to Mary. She checked the amount of the transaction and then handed the book back across the counter.

"There you go, Mrs. Summers. Have a nice weekend." Alison's stomach growled while Mrs. Summers carefully checked the new entry and then began the interminable process of collecting her belongings from the pile on the counter. It had been a mistake to skip lunch in the last-minute rush to buy the few small items she still needed before she left town. She hadn't even had time to eat the ham-and-cheese sandwich she had bought at the deli on the way back. It was still with her other purchases in the staff room.

She took a quick glance at the line and hoped she didn't get the swaying drunk who was one third of the way back. He wandered gently around in the space from which the other customers had withdrawn. Wearily, Alison pressed the button to summon the next customer and the green light above her head flashed on and off. She knew that if she didn't pay attention she could make a mistake which would cause her to miss the early bus to Vancouver. Thank God she had kept in touch with Sheila and that her old school friend had been so supportive. Without her encouragement to come out there and her offer to put her up until she found her way around, Alison would probably never have had the courage to go through with it. Her eyes again flicked towards the clock. Still only three thirty four.

The happy-looking young couple from the front of the line came eagerly towards her, and she switched the light off. Alison still didn't like the new system which channelled customers into one line-up for the next available teller. Most of the customers did though, since it wasted less of their time. No longer did they pick the shortest line only to get held up behind seemingly endless and convoluted transactions while others came later and left earlier. She still missed talking to the regulars whose faces, accounts and situations had become gradually familiar to her across the counter. The present system, which delivered customers to her wicket with the randomness of a bingo machine, left her with no regular customer contact, and usually managed to deprive her of the fleeting acquaintanceships she had built up over the years of occasional contact.

From their excited conversation she gathered that the couple, Tony and Holly Jackson, were off for a week's holiday in

Miami. Deftly she assembled the packages of U.S. traveller's cheques they requested, and she silently hoped that their trip to Florida would turn out better than the one she and Ted had taken about four years earlier. Her part of the transaction completed, she waited while they each signed their cheques, and she worried again whether the failure of the marriage had been her fault and whether she had made enough effort to save it. While the two happy Jacksons carefully stowed away their cheques, she wished them well and pressed the button to signal the next person in the seemingly endless line. Her stomach growled again.

The clock had advanced only eight more minutes towards the magic hour of four o'clock when she turned her attention to Herbert Maxwell and the bill-paying needs of the Maxwell family. Electricity, water, oil company, department store and credit card bills were automatically checked, verified and added. Her fingers flew across the calculator keys while her mind wandered again to Ted and his tightfisted control of their joint finances. At first it had seemed reasonable for his salary to be used to pay the mortgage and build up their joint nest-egg, while she used most of hers to pay the household expenses. It was only later, when they consolidated all their accounts to her branch in an effort to save on ever-increasing bank charges, that it sank in that not only was the house in his name, but that he was the sole signatory of the savings account. His reluctance to spend any money from the account had been the cause of too many long and unpleasant arguments between them, and his recent refusal to part with the money to let her buy the new carpets for the bedroom had been too much. Despite her careful management of the household expenses she was still more than a hundred dollars short of the money needed to take advantage of a sale at one of the local department stores. She had been determined that this time she would not dip into her own small personal savings account. "Let him keep the whole damned lot if it means so much to him," she thought. "It's worth it to be rid of him." A polite cough from Mr. Maxwell brought her back to the present. She handed over the receipted bills, wished him a pleasant weekend, glanced again at the crawling clock and pushed her button. Still another twelve minutes to closing time.

Arthur Peterson seemed to catapult himself towards the counter the second the light flashed. Whether this was to escape the drunk just behind him, or due to obvious impatience, Alison wasn't sure. Still yards away, he was already speaking rapidly as he advanced towards her, excitedly waving papers and cancelled cheques in front of him. The indignant and specific complaints about the errors in his current statement were, fortunately, beyond both her comprehension and responsibility. She tried to look interested in what he was saying, but from the corner of her eye she was watching the drunk weave his serpentine way towards

Vanessa at the far end of the counter. The combination of anxiety and hunger and the stuffy warmth of the bank had made her feel dizzy. Peterson was summarily referred to Nancy Brackett, the temporary accountant, who had the misfortune to be passing Alison's wicket at that moment. Mrs. Brackett had arrived only that morning as an emergency replacement for Mr. Johnson who had slipped on the icy pavement outside his house and broken his left leg. Although she had never been to this branch before, her forceful personality and quick humour had made her an instant success with the staff. Somehow she managed to simultaneously raise her eyebrows and roll her eyes at Alison as Peterson reiterated his complaints. Finally, and reluctantly, she escorted the irate man, his catalogue of the bank's delinquencies still being delivered at full spate, towards the back office for what promised to be a fierce, but relatively even, contest.

Alison watched them go but before she could press the button again his place had been taken by a short untidy man whose chin barely reached above the ledge of the counter. Julius Southport was probably her favourite customer. He had been one of the regulars at her wicket in the pre-lineup days and was unfailingly polite and considerate. He removed his old-fashioned black homburg to reveal a mass of grey, springy hair and regarded her gently.

"You look very tired, my dear," he said as he handed her a folded plastic supermarket bag and a sheet of paper. As usual the paper listed the amounts of the bundles of cash in the bag and their disbursement to his accounts.

"It's been a long week Mr. Southport. I'm fine really, and the end is almost here." She smiled while she opened the bag and checked the cash and slips.

Despite, or perhaps because of, his looking like a World War II refugee, he operated three small but successful, secondhand furniture stores in the downtown area. Several times a week he came in to deposit substantial sums of small notes into the several accounts he maintained at the branch, and she knew that his net worth was totally at odds with his disreputable appearance. Although she knew Mr. Southport to be a careful man and had never known him to make an error in his calculations, she counted and checked with her usual efficiency. As her fingers flicked through the piles of bills, her mind returned to the subject of Ted.

She had always been very tolerant of his faults, probably too tolerant, but her discovery that he was playing around had been the last straw. Ironically, she hadn't even suspected, and had only found out when she had gone to considerable effort on his behalf. He had said he had to take the car to drive to a late out-of-town business meeting one cold and miserable day last month. When she left work, despite her tiredness, she had impulsively decided to take the long bus ride to the East End Plaza to buy him the electric saw he had hinted he would like for his birthday. The trip had not started well. The bus had been jammed and the rain had begun the moment she got off at the plaza. From this unpromising beginning it had got even worse. Half the population of the city seemed to have crammed into the new hardware store to inspect the opening specials. When she had finally carried the heavy saw across the crowded, wet parking lot to the bus stop, she was exhausted, cold and miserable. The long day of standing at the bank counter and the crush of people in the store had taken its toll: she yearned for a hot bath and a gin and tonic.

The rain drummed on the plastic roof of the shelter and flowed in streams down the outside of the misty glass as she rubbed it hoping to see the bus. She envied the warm dry passengers in the traffic which stopped and started on the road outside. As yet another wave of cars hissed to rain-slicked stops at the traffic light, she had seen the familiar grey Oldsmobile with Ted in the driver's seat. Beside him was a young redhead whose sole aim at that moment seemed to be in devouring his right ear. Alison had pulled back into the darkest corner of the bus shelter. She stood there shaking while the light changed and the car surged away.

Automatically she stamped Mr. Southport's deposit slips and he politely tipped his battered hat, buttoned his black coat and wished her a good evening. As he departed, her hand reached automatically for the button.

She sneaked another glance at the clock as the next customer approached. Three fifty three -- still seven minutes until the doors were closed. She looked up at the tall smart-looking stranger who now stood at the wicket. From his stylish suit, well-cut hair and confident manner she decided he was probably a young executive on the way up to the boardroom of the insurance company building next door. He gave her a warm smile, took a savings account book from his inside jacket pocket and announced that he wished to close his account and take the balance in cash. She took the proffered passbook, looked at the withdrawal slip and noted the firm sloping signature of Edward Gunter. A wave of nausea and dizziness swept over her. She went towards the cabinet top behind her intending to verify the signature against the master account card, but didn't make it. After two or three unsteady steps she found it difficult to breathe and her head began to swim. She slumped down at a nearby desk, took several deep breaths, and tried desperately to concentrate.

"God, you look awful," said Nancy Brackett's concerned voice from above her. "What's the matter?"

"I'm okay," mumbled Alison. "I felt dizzy for a moment. I'll be fine in a second."

"What are you doing? Closing an account? I'll finish it for you," said Mrs. Brackett sweeping the withdrawal slip from Alison's hand. "Stay right there and rest for a minute." Briskly the accountant checked the signature against the account card, crossed to the terminal and inserted the passbook to wait for the automatic calculation of the current balance. While the machine chattered and spat she glanced with concern at Alison. Alison's stomach continued to churn and writhe while she watched the efficient conclusion of the transaction.

"There's another fifty three dollars and twelve cents interest, Mr. Gunter. Do you have any preference for the bills?" Mrs. Brackett asked as she wrote the balance onto the withdrawal slip, initialled it and handed the cancelled passbook back across the counter.

"Doesn't matter," he said, opening a smart brown wallet on the counter. "I'm buying a car tomorrow, and the sight of ready cash always seems to make them easier to deal with. Whatever's convenient."

The pile of bills totalling eight thousand two hundred and forty-two dollars was counted and recounted and the eighty-six cents in coins was taken from the cash drawer and pushed across the counter. The young man pocketed the coins and Alison continued to watch with interest as he casually threw the wallet into his monogrammed leather briefcase and snapped the locks shut. She smiled as he sauntered away and her eyes followed him across the bank to the street door. Mrs. Brackett abandoned the wicket, to the obvious annoyance of the young woman who had started towards her, and came over to check on Alison. Apparently reassured by what she saw, she made a few soothing noises and disappeared quickly towards the temporary refuge of the accountant's office.

Alison sat quite still for several minutes and stared blankly down at the desktop. She was totally unconscious of the other bank staff as they ebbed and flowed around her. When she finally raised her head she noted gratefully that the bank doors had been closed and locked and that one of the employees was now letting customers out.

The shortening line still shuffled hopefully forward within the containing ropes and the tellers seemed to find a last spurt of new energy now that the end of the week was in sight. Alison shook herself, returned to her position at the counter, and quickly took care of Bernice Walker's withdrawal of two hundred dollars. Judging by the pile of newspaper coupons the woman placed on the counter, most of the money would be back in the bank on Monday via the supermarket deposits. As the coupon clipper shuffled away she pressed the button again.

Gratefully she looked at what appeared to be her last customer. Jason Swenson was a small, earnest child who seemed to be about ten years old. He came to the wicket and solemnly announced that his grandmother had sent him to cash her social security cheque. Alison took the signed cheque and the accompanying note which he removed carefully from the battered envelope, smiled, stamped the cheque and counted out the money. When she had placed it in the envelope, she told him, gratuitously, to take it straight home and watched him as he walked confidently away after politely thanking her.

The line had gone and the empty ropes snaked towards the door across the dark red carpet which showed only the scuffs, scrapes and mud of the day's customers. She immediately started to clean up the papers on the countertop and began to balance her cash.

She did it slowly and for once it all came out correctly the first time. After a careful recheck she took the locked drawer to the vault, signed the register and headed for the staff rest room. After a brief visit to the washroom, where she saw a wan anxious face stare back at her from the mirror, she gathered her purse, coat and gloves from her locker and fought for space to put on her coat in the now-filling room. If she hurried she could still make the 4.30 bus and start her new Tedless life. Quickly she made sure that she had her money and ticket in her purse, then grabbed the brown leather suitcase and the shopping bag and headed for the door through the mass of chattering employees in their various stages of departure.

"Have a nice weekend, ladies," she called cheerfully as she went through the door.

A chorus of "Bye Alison", "So long", "Have a good weekend" and such polite, but insincere, rote phrases followed her out to the street.

She walked briskly as she threaded her way through the crowded streets and had soon covered the four blocks to the bus station. Pausing only briefly at the mailbox outside, she mailed the two carefully written letters, one to Ted and one to the Bank Manager, and arrived at the departure gate with minutes to spare. The reserved ticket she had purchased two days earlier was inspected, the driver took her suitcase, and she was soon settled into a window seat in the middle of the bus. She caught her reflection in the bus window and grinned at it. At last she'd done it! She reached into the shopping bag and took out the plastic-encased sandwich. As the rest of the passengers straggled on board, she removed the clinging wrapping from the sandwich and began to nibble at it slowly. The bus departed precisely on time and as it crawled through the downtown traffic Alison mentally toasted herself and her new start in Vancouver. This was probably the bravest thing she had ever done. It had been difficult to abandon almost all her clothes and possessions, and only the most precious and portable now sat in the baggage compartment beneath her feet. For once she wasn't even concerned about money. The contents of her small savings account and careful use of her one credit card should see her through until she could get a job. She supposed that her sudden departure would probably cause a ripple of speculation and concern at the bank on Monday, but mostly she wondered how much, if at all, Ted would really miss her.

Knowing him as she did she supposed that the loss of a somewhat boring overcautious wife would take second place to the other losses he must have incurred today. "How could he have managed to lose both wallet and briefcase?" she wondered. Probably he had left the car unlocked at the office parking lot, and the charming, and obviously enterprising, young man who said he wanted to buy the new car must have stolen them. Although their loss would be an annoyance, the disappearance of his savings would probably prove to be the most severe blow. She knew she really should have stopped the theft, but the unexpected opportunity to pay Ted back had been too much to resist. She had been tempted to verify the false signature on the withdrawal slip, let the young man walk away, and risk the consequences. However, thanks to Nancy Brackett's swift intervention during the fainting spell, there was no way anyone would be able to hold her responsible when the theft was discovered. "I almost wish I could be there to see his face when he finds out," thought Alison Gunter wryly as the bus to freedom laboured up the expressway ramp.

Eric Wright

Along with Ted Wood and Howard Engel, Eric
Wright is in large measure responsible for the
current international renaissance of Canadian
crime fiction. He's a three time winner of the
Crime Writers of Canada's Ellis Award, twice for
Best Novel and once for his short story
"Looking for an Honest Man" which appeared
in the Mosaic Press anthology *COLD BLOOD:
Murder in Canada*. His first novel, *The Night the
Gods Smiled*, introduced Charlie Salter of the
Metropolitan Toronto Police and in doing so won
not Wright's first Arthur Ellis Award, but also the
British Crime Writers Association's John
Creasey Award as the best first novel of 1983.
There are now six Salter adventures in print (the
third, *Death in the Old Country*, captured the
Arthur Ellis Award in 1986) and fans around the
world are devoted to the likable, incorruptible
detective. "Hephaestus" takes its title from the
name of a Greek god and it is, for Wright fans
used to Charlie Salter, a startling change of pace.

HEPHAESTUS

by Eric Wright

On the fourth day, Clayton was sitting with Jensen at the bar by the pool. They were watching the video of the day's picnic, an amateurish, incoherent production which was being received with huge enjoyment by the crowd at the bar, most of whom had been on the picnic, an excursion to an island round the bay, complete with barbecue, free wine and games. Everybody on the screen looked slightly drunk, and the games involved a lot of "mooning" as the celebrants competed to expose their bottoms to the camera. Occasionally the scene switched abruptly, and the audience at the bar howled with glee as they remembered what the camera could not show. The film ended amid applause and comments like, "Good thing that camera didn't come around our side of the island."

Jensen said, "You should have gone, Fred. I wonder if they set up a shrine to Dionysius?" He was a man in his early forties with a round, moon-like face and very large horn-rimmed glasses, who smiled constantly. Clayton had met him and his wife on the first day and stayed with them ever since because, like him, the Jensens had come for the peripheral activities, not to join in the organised fun. When Clayton first arrived at the vacation club and was greeted by the combination of summer camp and college pep rally with which the management made everyone feel at home -- group shenanigans which involved learning the club song, with gestures, and singing it every night to the setting sun -- he made a huge effort to keep his distance, refusing to wear a coloured ribbon to show which "team" he was on for the week, taking no part in Olympics day, and so on. The effort worked, for by the second day the Jolly Organisors, as the camp staff were known, began to leave him alone. Jensen made no effort at all. One look at the amusement on his balloon of a face, one remark -- "Ask the Leader if I may be excused the compulsory games if I attend the torch-light rally later, will you?" -- and they never bothered him again. Thereafter the three of them watched the highjinks on the beach, did not participate in the show put on by the Jolly Guests (the name the management gave the holidaying patrons), and avoided the disco altogether. By the third day there was an imaginary circle around the three of them, carved out by Jensen's stream of commentary, very vicious and very funny, on the activities of the other people. Occasionally Clayton experienced a twinge of discomfort when one of Jensen's remarks had an extra cutting edge. The Jolly Organisors who tried to involve them in the fun were trained to be cheery, and they would shrug at his response to them, smile and walk off, but they weren't either stupid or inhuman. Occasionally Clayton caught a glance from one of them that showed clearly enough that whatever their public face, they were very much aware of Jensen's contempt for them and their club. One incident in particular made Clayton nearly want to apologise for Jensen, distance himself from him. One of the Jolly Organisors was a man who called himself Kiki. Most of his duties consisted of clowning around, wearing outlandish costumes and pretending to "flash" the girls on the beach. One day Clayton and the Jensens were helping themselves to lunch, buffet-style. Part of the display was a label, "Lobster Salad". Beside it, an assistant chef invited the guests to help themselves, but when they lifted the lid of the pot, there was Kiki's head, grinning at them like a decapitated lunatic. It was quite a shock -- Kiki had a very powerful grin -- and it caused a lot of hilarity. Jensen saw the joke from another part of the dining-room before he could get caught by it. Clayton watched him fill up his plate with macaroni salad, and approach the pot, looking innocent. When he lifted the lid and saw Kiki, he reacted in mock dismay and dumped his salad all over Kiki's head. Everyone else thought his was a wonderful, accidental reaction, the best yet, but Clayton was watching Kiki as the chef cleaned off his head, and his eyes were on Jensen. Then he looked at Clayton, very briefly, but for long enough to make Clayton wish he wasn't such a well-known Jensenite. But in the end, Clayton laughed with Jensen, preferring to be in the circle with Jensen and his wife rather than outside on his own.

Why had they come? For the tennis, Jensen told Clayton. The club's major daytime activity was tennis, and Cynthia was an avid player, like Clayton. And like Clayton, the Jensens were curious about what these places were really like. Tennis was both the reason and an excuse.

Cynthia Jensen was at least ten years younger than her husband, an attractive blonde made slightly too thin by the amount of exercise she took and by her devotion to fruit-juice instead of food. While she played tennis, Jensen went for walks with his camera -- he had several of them including a movie camera -- and sometimes he swam in the pool, though he was self-conscious about exposing himself because he never sun-bathed and when he took his clothes off, all the golden bodies got some revenge for the contempt he had for them when he was dressed.

Clayton joined them for brunch after the morning's tennis, and they idled the day away together until it was time for the five-o'clock session. They stuck together for meals because it was

the only defence against the club practice of mixing up the guests for
different tables at every meal, a custom which meant that on the
first night Clayton ate with seven French people who ignored him,
and the Jensens ate with a group of weight-lifters from Chicago
who, Jensen said, could have earned their living in English movies
as stock American boors. The three of them spent their time on the
beach. Jensen assumed Clayton was of their party from the start,
and spoke as if the three of them were on Mars, trying to make
sense of the native inhabitants. The other guests were not entirely
homogeneous. The superb tennis facilities attracted a fair number
who came for that alone, and on one occasion Clayton fell in with
four psychologists from New York who were very good company
after hours. But Jensen wanted no part of any larger group. He
needed Clayton as someone to enjoy his misanthropy, and a larger
audience would have recoiled from him, and perhaps even
defanged him. Jensen was like the kind of father who can create
attitudes within a house, tyrannise it with his world view, but when
the family takes an excursion the children realise that strangers
are impervious to their father's influence, that there are other ways
of seeing and dealing with the world. So the father tries to keep the
children prisoners at home rather than risk any diminution of his
influence. Jensen was like that. Once Clayton was accepted, he
was assumed to share Jensen's every attitude. Clayton
understood this and let it happen. Jensen's was very funny; he
suited Clayton for a week, as did his wife. All of them were getting
what they came for.

Cynthia was not in Clayton's tennis group. The players were
graded from one to six, according to ability, and Cynthia was a
three, whereas Clayton was a four. They played at the same time,
learning the same skills but at different levels. On the first night
Clayton went to the disco, but once he had met the Jensens he never
bothered again. (Jensen said, "I only go to discos to exercise my
wife"). Cynthia said very little. She played tennis, read best-
sellers, and smiled at the stream of entertaining malice that ema-
nated from her husband. Clayton hadn't spent many hours in their
company before he was speculating about them, but he gained no
clue to their relationship. Jensen discouraged chat about private
matters. It suited him to treat Clayton as a mutual observer of the
mating games that were being played around them, but he never
introduced a personal note.

Inevitably they talked about the reputation of the club and
whether it was living up to it. Cynthia and Clayton were up early,
and they could confirm that at dawn not a few souls were
criss-crossing the grounds on their way home. Jensen was a very
close observer of the way partnerships shifted between one day
and the next. He was particularly interested in one couple from the
Mid-West whom he overheard telling others that this was the

eleventh club they had stayed at. This couple prowled along the shore, hand in hand, scanning the beach as though looking for a lost child. On the third day they found another couple and were hardly seen again.

And then, on the fourth day, the world changed. Clayton hadn't played tennis that afternoon, and he and Jensen were awaiting the arrival of Cynthia after her game. Jensen looked at Clayton after the video of the picnic ended and said, "Cynthia is having an affair, if that is the word for it."

Clayton waited for the joke, but none came. "When?" he asked, eventually, after he had got his breath back. "She's either playing tennis or with us."

"When she is supposed to be playing tennis," Jensen said, "she's fornicating."

"Who with ?"

"One of the tennis pros, I think."

"The tennis pros spend all their time on the court," Clayton said. "There is no way."

Jensen shook his head. "They get time off," he said. "Perhaps she is fornicating with all of them, one at a time." His demeanour, like his tone of voice, was unchanged. He might have been discussing any of the guests. "Haven't you noticed? When she is supposed to be playing tennis, she's not always there."

"She isn't in my group," Clayton reminded him.

"Right. So you wouldn't notice. This morning I followed her down to the court where she was supposed to be playing. She wasn't there. The pro, rat faced boy with yellow hair, said he hadn't seen her since the first day. She is fornicating with someone. Playing the two-backed beast."

"How do you know?"

"What possible other reason could there be?"

Cynthia appeared on the other side of the pool and waved to them.

"What are you going to do?" Clayton asked.

"I don't know yet. This picnic has given me an idea though."

His wife approached and he stopped talking. When she arrived, sweaty, with a small blister on her thumb, Clayton looked at Jensen to see if he doubted that at least on this occasion she had been playing tennis.

"Have a good game, dear?" Jensen asked.

"The best since I arrived." She plopped down into a chair at the side of him.

"Why don't you give Fred here a game?"

"We're not in the same group." Cynthia stood up. "I need a drink," she said and walked over to the bar.

Clayton had no need to think. Under the circumstances, he had to act, to warn her about her husband. He followed her to the bar on the pretext of needing another drink himself. There was no time to introduce the subject gently. "Your husband thinks you are having an affair," he said.

She looked at him as if he had made a joke. "Does he, indeed? Who with?"

"A tennis pro, maybe."

That was all they had time for, but it was enough. He had done his duty, and now it was up to her. They walked back to Jensen, and she sat down and reached to push back a bit of hair that was sticking out over one of Jensen's ears. That was it, for then, and the evening passed like all the others. When Cynthia had changed, they ate dinner, watched a series of sketches put on by the Jolly Organisors, and went to bed.

The next morning Clayton got up a little earlier than usual and stood among the trees, watching the Jensens' door. Cynthia appeared, in tennis clothes, and started off towards the courts. Shortly afterwards Jensen came out with a camera hung from his shoulder, but instead of following his wife, he struck off along a path that led over the hill to a village around the other side of the cliffs. He seemed uninterested in Cynthia, or where she was going, and Clayton wondered as he followed her towards the courts, if he was getting a glimpse of a very strange marriage.

After lunch the three of them were sitting by the pool, drinking coffee, watching an advertisement for a sailing excursion that was being shown on the video screen. Cynthia picked up her beach bag and Clayton got ready to join them in a walk down to the beach. Jensen put a hand on his arm. "You go ahead, Cynthia," he said. "I want to tell Fred a dirty joke I heard this morning."

She wrinkled her nose in mock disgust as she walked away. Jensen turned to Clayton. "I've thought of a way to get my revenge on Cynthia," he said. The sun sparkled on his glasses. "The video we were watching yesterday gave me an idea. Do you know the story of Hephaestus?"

Jensen was a broker of some kind, but he had had a good education, and he enjoyed playing the role of the scholar, stuffing his conversation with literary and classical allusions. One day as they were watching the parachute skiers climb the sky, he compared them to Icarus, wondering which one would get too near the sun, hoping he would be there when it happened.

"No," Clayton said. "Who was Hephaestus?"

"You may know him as Vulcan."

"The god of rubber tires?"

For a moment, all of Jensen's contempt was focussed on Clayton. "No," he said. "The smith-god. He made fabulous armour for the other gods, that sort of thing. He was married to Aphrodite. Now Aphrodite was unfaithful with Ares, the god of war -- a lecher and a braggart, by the way -- and Helios the sun-god saw them at it and told Hephaestus. Hephaestus then fashioned a very strong, very thin net, which he hung over his bed. The next time that Aphrodite and Ares came together Hephaestus dropped the net, catching them in the middle of the act and making it impossible for them to move. Then Hephaestus invited all the gods over to look. How the gods laughed."

"What has all this to do with Cynthia?"

"Let's go for a little walk. I'll show you."

He took them along the path that Clayton had seen him take that morning, away from the tennis courts, over the hill, and then through some scrub until they reached the cliff edge. They had walked through two hundred and seventy degrees and were now on the other side of the tennis courts, looking down at the beach. About fifty years along the cliff path he stopped. "Look down there," he said.

Clayton looked and saw an indentation in the cliff-face like a huge mine-shaft with a deep crack down the side. The eye was led down the shaft to a patch of sand that was nearly enclosed by the cliff. As they watched, a couple came along and climbed over the rocks, through the gap in the cliff face to the patch of sand inside. The shadows at the bottom were too deep to see who they were, but what they were doing was obvious enough. It was a perfect love-nest.

"What has all this to do with Cynthia?" Clayton asked.

"I overheard some people talking about this place. I put two and two together and it seemed possible that Cynthia knew about it."

"So?"

"Hephaestus." Jensen tapped his camera. "Instead of a net I have this."

"You intend to take pictures of Cynthia making love? Have you seen her?"

"Oh, yes. I've seen her all right. Look through this." He handed Clayton his camera.

Through the view-finder, the same scene was visible, perfectly framed by the circle of rock.

"You can't see who it is," Clayton said. "It's too dark."

"Not in the morning. The sun comes up there..." Jensen pointed out to sea, "...and it sends a powerful shaft of light into the cave about eight o'clock. When my Aphrodite and Ares are locked in each other's arms, Helios himself is on his way south."

Clayton realized then the monstrous plan that Jensen had devised. "You are going to photograph them, and show it on the camp video?"

"I'm not going to. I have." He pointed to the camera that Clayton was still holding, and reached for it.

Clayton snatched the camera back and Jensen lunged for it and stumbled. He fell forward and Clayton twisted to keep the camera out of his reach, then stiff-armed him to keep him from grabbing at Clayton's trousers as he fell. Jensen disappeared over the edge, falling like Icarus, not to the sea, but to the rocks below.

Clayton stood staring at Jensen's descent, and two Jolly Organisors came out of the bushes, Kiki and the rat-faced tennis pro with the yellow hair.

"I'll take the camera," Kiki said. "Now tell us what happened."

Clayton told them: Jensen and he were taking a walk and Jensen had fallen over the edge as Clayton got ready to take his picture with his own camera. "It was an accident," he said.

The Jolly Organisors looked at each other. "This could get complicated," Kiki said. "Okay, you were up here taking pictures, and he took an extra step backwards. Okay?" Kiki looked at Clayton, and continued to speak slowly. "That's what happened. Okay? Danny and I were walking along here. We saw it all. You were twenty feet away from him. Right, Danny?"

Danny nodded and turned away.

Kiki walked to the edge of the cliff. "He was *here* and you were *there.* Okay?"

Clayton stared at him gratefully. "It wasn't my fault," he started to say, but Kiki cut him off.

"How could it be? You were twenty feet apart." He waited until he was sure that Clayton understood.

"What were you doing here?" Clayton asked.

"That's easy. See that guy?" Kiki pointed to a figure floating high above the sea, dangling from a parachute. "Danny was up there this morning and he thought he saw a Peeping Tom, taking pictures down the tunnel of love. That's the local name for it. So when we noticed you two heading this way with a camera, we decided to take a look."

Down below the beach was full of people; faces were turned up looking at them.

"You were *there* and he was *here,*" Kiki said. "Okay?"

"You know what he was doing?" Clayton said. "He was spying on his wife, taking pictures of her."

"Let's go down now," Kiki said, cutting him off. "And shut up."

It stayed that simple. There was a routine investigation and a verdict of accidental death. Someone fell off a cliff while he was taking pictures.

Clayton never saw Cynthia again because she left with her husband's body, but he stayed around and played tennis all he could for the last two days. On the last night, as he was thinking about going to bed, Kiki came up to him at the bar. "Some of the Organisors are having a party tonight," he said. "In Danny's room. Why don't you join us?"

Clayton was astonished and very pleased. About an hour later he made his way to the staff quarters where seven or eight of the Organisors were drinking beer and listening to music. It seemed to be a stag party, which surprised Clayton. He took a beer from Danny and made himself at home. Soon the reason for the absence of any girls was made clear as someone switched on the television screen and the pornographic movies began.   The Organisors cheered and derided the performances in a couple of small films, then Kiki said, "The next one is special."

It was an amateur effort, jumpy and awkwardly filmed, like the picnic video, but the images were clear enough. It began with a shot of Cynthia walking along the beach in her tennis shorts and then disappearing into the cave in the cliff. The next shot was straight down the shaft, focussing on the patch of white sand now brilliantly lit, where Cynthia's lover was waiting. Soon they were naked and the camera zoomed down on the wriggling pair. His face was obscured at first, but in the natural course of things the camera caught a frontal view as he lay back with his hands behind his head. Even Clayton's appendectomy scar was clearly visible.

He made for the door but Kiki was already in the doorway. "We always have a party on Friday nights for a few of the guests," he said. "Have a good trip home."

That was two years ago. They move those organisors around a lot so that now, whenever he hears of anyone who has spent a week at one of the clubs, Clayton always wonders, was Kiki there, and was there a party on the last night, and how long does a videotape last? Forever?

Charlotte MacLeod

Charlotte MacLeod was born in Bath, New Brunswick in 1922 and now lives in rural Maine. Since 1978, she's published over 20 mystery novels. Among her most popular books are those about Peter Shandy, a professor at Balaclava Agricultural College. The first Shandy Novel, *Rest You Merry*, is a delightful Christmas mystery, and *The Corpse in Oozak's Pond* was nominated for an Edgar Award in 1988 as the best mystery novel of the year. Under her pen name, Alisa Craig, she also writes mysteries set in Ontario and her native New Brunswick. She was the guest of honour at Bouchercon XIX, the International Crime Writing Conference held in San Diego in 1988. "A Tale of a Tub" is a prime example of the best in her work, combining wit, humour and a cast of eccentric and memorable characters.

A TALE OF A TUB

by Charlotte MacLeod

"Oh, cripes! There he goes again. I wonder who's dyin' this time."

Well might Jedediah Olson ask. Ever since they'd hired the new minister of the Deliverance Church, a deathbed baptism in Pitcherville meant another thank-you job for Jeb. He was not the sexton nor yet the gravedigger, he was the town blacksmith, as his father had been before him. But Jed moved with the times. He was also the town plumber, when he had anything to plumb.

This didn't happen often, since the revolutionary concept of running water inside the house had not yet really taken hold in some of New Brunswick's smaller communities. In Pitcherville there were to be sure, several sinks with faucets and drains and no fewer than three flush closets standing as testaments to Jed's more recently acquired skills. However, it was the Reverend Strongitharm Goodheart's self-filling and self-emptying bathtub that Jed had considered his chef d'oeuvre when he'd installed it in the Deliverance parsonage some eighteen months previously. Since that time Jed had developed a personal grudge against the minister's bathtub.

Strongitharm Goodheart, be it said, had heard the call to the ministry at the age of seventeen and a half, while he was in the midst of plowing a furrow on his father's farm out back of Little Pitcher. Once having put his hand to a different plow, he turned not back but finished his furrow, unhitched the horses, and headed straight for the Deliverance seminary with his mother's kiss on his brow and her willingly bestowed egg money in his pocket.

His father's blessing had been given with some secret unwillingness, for Strongitharm had always more than lived up to his name around the farm. He did express the generous opinion that his son would be a credit to the family, and was right. Strongitharm flung himself into his new studies with the same zeal he'd shown in cultivating the lower forty. Once ordained, he'd wearied not in welldoing. All things considered, the Pitcherville deacons agreed, they might have gone farther and fared worse, even though Mr. Goodheart, as he must now be respectfully known, did seem to have picked up some awfully advanced notions along with his higher education.

That a Deliverance minister should be ready, able and even delighted to go any distance in any weather at any hour to snatch a dying brand from the burning didn't surprise them any; this was just one more duty that went with the job. That he should insist on baptizing by immersion excited no remark, he wouldn't have lasted long at Pitcherville Deliverance if he didn't.

What was different about Strongitharm Goodheart was the way he chose to cope with the frequent logistical difficulties presented by iced-over ponds, frozen rivers, and (depending on the season) dried-up streams.

His method was to unhook his bathtub from its pipes, carry it downstairs on his back, lash it across the back of his Model T Ford, and drive to the house of the afflicted with the tub clattering and banging behind him. He would then lug it to the bedside and personally pump enough buckets to fill it. He'd add a few kettlefuls of boiling water to temper the chill, for Strongitharm was a kindly man, and get on with what he'd been called to do.

Strongitharm Goodheart was probably the only minister in the Maritimes who'd have had the ingenuity to think of taking the bathtub along, the zeal to attempt it, and the physical strength to carry it; but he was a humble man withal and knew his limitations. He couldn't plumb worth a hoot. Therefore, once the petitioner had been duly immersed, prayed over, dried off, and sent rejoicing on his or her way to recovery or the Pearly Gates as the case might be, Strongitharm would chauffeur his bathtub back home, carry it up to the bathroom, and send for Jed Olson to hook it up again.

The minister always offered to pay, but Jed would never take a cent. He knew Mr. Goodheart made barely enough to live on and if by a miracle there was anything left over from feeding and clothing the minister's wife and child, it went to succour the needy or buy small comforts for the aged and infirm. Jed knew his own wife would skin him if he exacted payment for helping out with the Lord's work, and Jed knew that doing a favour would give him a perfect excuse to worm the details out of the minister before anybody else did. Naturally the hangers-on around the smithy looked to Jed as their oracle and naturally they expected him to come through with the goods now.

"I heard old Mrs. Saltmarsh was slipping fast," one ventured to get the ball rolling.

Jed shrugged off Mrs. Saltmarsh. "She wouldn't need baptizin'. She's been saved ever since right after she buried 'er second husband. Ought seven I think it was. Old Hosea Doright, that travelin' evangelist who used to come around, baptized 'er after one of 'is revival meetin's. I remember my father tellin' about it. It was in April an' cold as a stepmother's kiss. The river was runnin' awful high an' when Hosea shoved 'er under the current swept 'er out of 'is hands an' carried 'er downstream till she fetched up on a snag.

An' Hosea just stood there yellin', 'The Lord giveth an' the Lord taketh away. Pass me another.' Hosea was a good man, my father said, but he had an awful one-track mind. By gorry, look at that, he's stoppin' right in front of Wilt's Drygoods Store."

"You don't s'pose Miser Wilt's finally goin' to get a bath?"

That was indeed a point for speculation. James Wilt, who lived in the flat over his store and in fact owned the entire building, had a phobia against catching cold. He didn't bathe more than once or twice a year. It was whispered among the cognoscenti that he sewed himself into his Stanfield's double knits on the first day of September every year and didn't take out the stitches till the last day of June. Wilt was not a person to get close to and not many tried, for his disposition was no more ingratiating than his personal habits.

The only two people who had to suffer Wilt's presence at close quarters were his downtrodden housekeeper, a worthy widow lady named Mary Higbed, and his equally if not more downtrodden nephew. Perce Wilt had come to his uncle as an orphan at the age of twelve and been put straight to work learning the drygoods business at a wage of five cents a week plus his room and board. Perce was now thirty-two years old and had been upped, rumor had it, to five dollars a month.

Perce would no doubt fall heir one day to the Wilt fortune. The old man did well out of the store. He let Perce wait on the customers, which was probably an excellent idea, considering, while he himself ran a successful wholesale business in notions and yard goods out of the basement. James never sold on credit and never spent a cent he didn't have to. He'd skin a flea for its hide and tallow. He was generally supposed to keep his money, all in gold pieces, in an asbestos lined sack under his bed so he'd have it handy to take with him when his time came to go where he was surely headed. Only now that Mr. Goodheart was on the scene, perdition might not be quite so certain.

"Has to be either Wilt or Mrs. Higbed," said one of the boys. "Perce is too young to die."

"I dunno," said another. "Perce's been lookin' awful peaked lately."

"He's stuck on the new schoolteacher," Jed Olson spoke with the voice of authority as usual, "an' his uncle won't give 'im time off to go courtin', much less enough of a raise to set up housekeepin' on. They'd have to live up there with the old man an' what good-lookin' young woman in 'er right mind would settle for Wilt an' his underwear?"

"All right then," said the first speaker, "Maybe Perce pined away or hung himself or somethin'. It's got to be one of 'em. Nobody else ever goes there 'cept a traveler now an' then."

Traveling drygoods salesmen did endure the mephitic presence of James Wilt more bravely than most because, whiffy though he might be and hard bargainer though he assuredly was, Wilt bought big and he paid cash on the button. Occasionally one of them even stayed overnight in the flat, there being no commercial lodging available in Pitcherville and trains being few and far between.

To a salesman with an insensitive nose, a night with Wilt was probably no hardship. Mrs. Higbed was reputed to keep the flat neat as a pin and set a reasonably good table considering the meagerness of her housekeeping allowance. Wilt had, as Jed was able to inform the know-it-all who insisted on keeping the number of possibles down to three, a traveler staying with him right now; that good-looking fellow with the big blond mustache who traveled in knitting needles and had stayed a few times before. He'd attended the church social last night and been observed giving the new schoolteacher a glad eye, to Perce Wilt's obvious discomfiture.

This was all very interesting, but Jed had a wagon tire to straighten. Once they'd all watched Mr. Goodheart carry in the bathtub, he put the bellows to the forge and reached for his hammer. The spectators went about their own affairs. Up over the shop, the minister was attending to his.

He'd found Mrs. Higbed in a terrible taking. Mr. Wilt, she'd informed him, had an awful pain in his chest and could not get his breath. He was dying and he knew it, therefore he wasn't about to waste good money on the doctor. He hadn't even wanted the minister until Mrs. Higbed had quoted a few passages she remembered from Hosea Doright's revival meeting and taken it upon herself to see that he had a fighting chance to escape The Bad Place.

"Mr. Wilt's not a bad man, Mr. Goodheart," she all but sobbed. "Truly he isn't. People just have a spite against him because he's a little bit near with his money and doesn't always smell very nice. You'll do what you can for him, won't you?"

"I'm only the instrument, Mrs. Higbed," Strongitharm reminded her gently. "Come along, let's get some water heating. Where's Perce?"

"Downstairs in the store, as usual. Perce has to be there by half-past six to sweep out, clean the stove, lug out the ashes and all that. His uncle has always been strict about opening on time, with everything in order. But I mustn't stand here gossiping when the poor soul may be drawing his last breath, for all we know. You take the bathtub straight in there, Mr. Goodheart, and I'll see to the water."

Strongitharm was glad to put down the tub, backpacking it up a long flight of stairs hadn't been easy. He set it down as gently as he could and bent over the old man, trying to remember not to breathe.

"How are you feeling, Mr. Wilt?"

The drygoods magnate had several quilts tucked over him, all of them spotlessly clean. Only his arms were outside, covered by a dark gray flannel nightshirt. As the minister spoke, Wilt raised his right hand and clutched feebly at that portion of the quilt under which his chest presumably lay.

"Heart," he gasped. "Pain. Awful. Can't -- get -- breath. Going -- to -- die."

"Going to glory, Mr. Wilt." Strongitharm took the cold, palsied hand in his own warm one and began to recite the Twenty-Third Psalm. He continued speaking words of hope and comfort until he judged the water was warm, then went to help Mrs. Higbed with the kettles.

"Perhaps you'd better ask Perce to come up," he told her gently. "Someone mentioned last night at the social that you also have an overnight visitor?"

"Mr. Ham," she replied. "He's just finishing his breakfast. He slept in this morning because the down train's not due for another half hour."

"Is Mr. Ham a close friend of Mr. Wilt?"

"Close as any, I suppose."

"Then you may as well get him, too."

Mrs. Higbed had left off trying to hide her tears. "I'll break it to them gently."

By the time the bathtub was filled, the three were assembled around it, Mrs. Higbed sniffling into her apron in a subdued and ladylike way, Perce looking somber and worried, Mr. Ham putting on a decent show of grief for an old and valued customer. Strongitharm bent over the bed, laid back the covers, and raised up the feeble body.

As he did so, his hand encountered a patch of dampness on the left breast of the nightshirt. That struck him as being rather odd. Mr. Wilt must have spilled something on himself quite recently, though Mrs. Higbed had mentioned while they were dealing with the kettles that her employer had taken neither bite nor sip since last night's supper. He hadn't been out of bed, he would hardly have asked for a wash basin to be brought to him.

The dampness was puzzling, but hardly important at such a time as this. Murmuring appropriate words, Strongitharm eased his current penitent into the baptismal font. Knowing Mr. Wilt's personal habits, he's expected the warm water to turn colour a bit. What he had not anticipated was the reddish stain that began to spread out from the region of James Wilt's chest. "Merciful Heaven!" he exclaimed, "He's bleeding!"

"But how can he be?" gasped Mrs. Higbed.

"I don't know, but we've got to find out. Let's put him back on the bed. Here, Perce, help me get this nightshirt off."

"You won't want us." Mr. Ham was backing toward the door. "Come on, Mrs. Higbed."

"No, stay," ordered Strongitharm in a tone that brooked no disobediance. "One of you hand me a jackknife or something."

Perce had a penknife with a cork stuck on the tip. Strongitharm took the cork off and began to rip stitches out of the old man's underwear, ignoring the nephew's startled cry, "But it's only March!"

Soon the bare chest lay exposed, dingy and greasy and showing a few unlovely wisps of wet gray hair. Below and slightly to the left of the nipple, a hardly discernible puncture wound oozed a tiny trickle of fresh blood. Strongitharm inspected it closely, then straightened up.

"Mr. Wilt, you've been stabbed, with a long, thin, pointed weapon. Mrs. Higbed, please get the doctor, and the constable."

"Too late," gasped the victim. "My heart --"

"Your heart's working fine." Strongitharm had his hand on Wilt's wrist now, counting the pulse. "Your would-be murderer made the customary layman's mistake of thinking your heart was on your left side. Actually it's in the middle. What you have, Mr. Wilt, is a punctured lung. It's causing you a lot of pain and making it hard to breathe, but it's not likely to kill you if you're properly taken care of. Even if the wound doesn't heal right, you do have another lung, you know."

"I do?"

"Oh yes, everybody does, one on each side. Now, Mrs. Higbed, if you'll take this union suit away and bring in a washrag, some soap, and a clean towel, we'll give Mr. Wilt a nice, warm bath so he'll be ready when the doctor gets here. I'll finish the baptism at the same time. The Lord won't mind if we kill two birds with one stone."

"Never -- mind -- the -- birds," wheezed James Wilt. "Who -- killed -- me?"

"First things first, Mr. Wilt. I want you to stay perfectly still and not talk any more till the doctor comes."

The constable was first on the scene. He panted into the room shouting, "Where's the jeezledy bugger that murdered Mr. Wilt?"

By now the patient was back in bed, clean as a whistle and with a hint of colour in his cheeks.

"He's not dead," the nephew stammered. "See?"

"Don't make a particle o' difference. I got to take you in anyways, Perce, it's my duty. I know why you done it. You wanted your uncle's money so's you could marry the schoolteacher. You didn't dare wait any longer 'cause Mr. Ham here was fixin' to cut you out. What did you stab 'im with? One o' them spike files like they use down to the drugstore to poke the prescriptions onto, eh?"

"We don't have a spike file in the store. Uncle James thinks they're a waste of money. We just put a rock on top of the papers and keep the windows shut."

"Huh, a likely story! All right, then, what did you use? You'll have to tell the high sheriff anyway, so you might as well tell me."

"Ingrate," muttered Miser Wilt, carefully so as not to strain his punctured lung and run up the doctor's bill.

"Judge not, Mr. Wilt," said Strongitharm Goodheart, who had been doing some prayerful cogitating since Mrs. Higbed's departure. "Remember you'll still have to answer to your Maker some day, like the rest of us. I don't believe it's going to be your nephew who'll show up before the Throne with blood on his hands."

"Sorry, Mr. Goodheart, but I think you're kind o' squeezin' out a little too much milk of human kindness here," said the constable, not liking to contradict the minister but still trying to do his duty as he saw it. "If it ain't Perce, who else could it be?"

"Yes, who?" demanded Mrs. Higbed and the doctor, who had by now arrived on the scene.

"The explanation is quite obvious, I should think, Strongitharm replied. "Mr. Wilt, where do you keep your money? If you want to keep your nephew out of jail, you'd better tell me now."

James Wilt gasped a few times to indicate that he either could not or would not tell. With that, the indomitable though modest Mrs. Higbed stepped forward.

"If Mr. Wilt won't tell and it's a matter of saving the good name of an innocent young man who won't even swat a fly without apologizing to it first and has been a good and faithful nephew ever since he entered this house as an orphan boy of twelve, then I'll tell you myself, not that I'm one to snoop but I couldn't have mopped this floor twice a week faithful for the past twenty-seven years and four months without knowing about the loose board right under your bathtub, Mr. Goodheart, which if you'll move it I'll show you where the money's hidden as is my Christian duty and Mr. Wilt will forgive me because he's a good man at heart no matter what anybody says."

"I'll get a bailing bucket," said the constable, no longer a flaming angel of vengeance. "No sense straining our guts lifting all that water."

The water was dumped, the tub was moved, the hiding place revealed. And it was empty! James Wilt was all set to have a relapse and the doctor to snatch him back from the jaws of death for a tidy fee when Strongitharm intervened.

"Just what I expected. Constable, consider the facts. Perce Wilt is no dumbbell or he wouldn't be able to run the drygoods store the way he does. If he'd been guilty of attacking his uncle, he'd have had sense enough to leave the money where it was and make a sham of discovering it after Mr. Wilt died, when he'd have inherited it anyway."

"The minister's right," said the doctor. "He's right about the punctured lung, too, Mr. Wilt. We'll have you back inside that union suit in a few weeks, provided whoever stabbed you the first time doesn't take another whack. Who did it, Mr. Goodheart?"

"Well, doctor, when I lifted Mr. Wilt out of bed, I felt a wet spot on his nightshirt. Right about here." The minister demonstrated. "Look, here's a round hole just about the size of the wound in his chest. That proves he was stabbed through his nightshirt and all. The would-be murderer then sponged the nightshirt to get rid of the small bloodstain left when the weapon was pulled out, evidently hoping the puncture would never be noticed and the death would be put down to natural causes. But underneath his nightshirt, Mr. Wilt was also wearing his heavy winter underwear, which naturally got more blood on it than the nightshirt did."

"That's why the water turned pink when you put him in the tub," said Mrs. Higbed in awe and wonderment. "But who would wash away a small stain on top and leave a big one underneath?"

"Only someone who didn't know Mr. Wilt always sewed himself into his winter underwear and never took it off till spring. That means it had to be somebody from out of town, but also somebody who'd stayed here often enough to have found out where Mr. Wilt hid his money. Somebody who not only carried a piece of luggage big enough to hide the gold in, but also dealt in long, thin, pointed objects. If you search Mr. Ham's sample case, constable, I expect you'll find both Mr. Wilt's missing money and a large-sized steel knitting needle that's been sharpened to a dagger point."

"Well, I'll be --" the constable caught Strongitharm Goodheart's stern eye upon him, gulped, and added "blessed. Mr. Ham, you're under --"

From over by the depot came a long, dismal hoot. It was the morning train. With a mighty thrust of his arm, Mr. Ham hurled the constable into the now empty tub, fled from the house and, as they soon learned, leaped on the train in the nick of time. He had perforce left his sample case behind. It contained, as Strongitharm had predicted, a Number Six knitting needle that had been sharpened to a deadly weapon and all Mr. Wilt's hidden hoard except for thirty silver dollars that the scoundrel must have put straight in his pocket. Ham had in fact jangled a good deal as he'd run away, Mrs. Higbed recalled.

James Wilt took his loss in surprisingly good part. He followed the doctor's orders, tenderly nursed by the ever-loyal Mrs. Higbed. He made a fine recovery and paid his bill to the doctor without even trying to deduct two per cent for cash on the button. On the first Saturday night after the doctor had pronounced him fit to be out and about, he showed up at the parsonage with a fresh cake of soap in his hand and a clean suit of underwear over his arm and requested permission to use the minister's bathtub. When he departed after scrupulously washing out the ring, he was discovered to have left a five-dollar gold piece in the soap dish. On Sunday morning he appeared in church with Mrs. Higbed, freshly barbered and smelling only of bay rum. To the wonder of all beholders, he put a dollar in the plate.

These weekly ablutions continued. So did the gold pieces, not to mention the dollars in the plate. With these important additions to his formerly pitiful income, Strongitharm Goodheart was able not only to step up his charitable works among the aged, the ailing, and the indigent, but also to keep his growing brood of happy, well-behaved little Goodhearts in shoes, porridge, and slate pencils, and to buy his beloved wife her first new hat in fourteen years.

Mrs. Goodheart soon had occasion to show off her hat at a fashionable society wedding, as she watched her beaming husband unite in holy wedlock Perce Wilt and the beautiful schoolteacher. For a wedding present, Perce and his bride received the avuncular blessing and full partnership in both the retail and the wholesale ends of the drygoods business. Shortly thereafter, James himself visited the parsonage with a blushing Mrs. Higbed on his arm to request a similar though quieter service for himself and the woman who alone of all in Pitcherville had seen the real man under the overworked union suit.

James Wilt was never heard to repine his stolen thirty pieces of silver. He never tried to find out what had happened to the treacherous Mr. Ham. Vengeance was the Lord's, Strongitharm Goodheart had assured him, and James was content to leave the job to the One best equipped to handle it.

Mel D. Ames

Mel Ames was born in Winnipeg in the twenties. After six years in the army and airforce during World War II, he went into the advertising business in Toronto. Later he moved to the west coast and sold his first story to *Ellery Queen's Mystery Magazine* in 1968. Mel's most popular creation is Cathy Carruthers, the Amazoonian police detective whose investigations centre around such bizarre victims such as Santa Claus; a man crucified on a church lawn and several department store mannequins. The first Carruthers novelet appeared in *Mike Shayne Mystery Magazine* in November 1980 and she soon became one of *MSMM's* most popular recurring characters. "The Devil Made Me Do It" is the first new Carruthers adventure in five years. Her admirers have cause for celebration.

THE DEVIL MADE ME DO IT

by Mel D. Ames

Night watchman Otis Scroggs, padded his way stolidly down the short hallway behind the concession stand in Metro Central's Memorial Arena. A glance at his watch told him it was forty-seven minutes after three a.m.. He was on schedule, in spite of the ugly hue and cry that had arisen in the wake of the *Messiah's* resounding victory over his arch foe, *Satan*, in the pro-wrestling main event. Fans and wrestlers alike, of both good and evil bias, had been seemingly bent on one last glorious moment of mayhem before reluctantly vacating the Arena. But now, amid the shambles, and in the deserted building's eerie hush, Otis felt grimly alone as he approached his tenth and final check point. There was meagre comfort in the knowledge that each rendezvous point on his round of the huge sports facility, including this one, was under constant surveillance by closed-circuit television.

The security phone was midway along the hall, in full view of the camera and directly across from a small walk-in freezer. The freezer was used communally by the concession stand (for the preservation of food), and by a never-ending flux of professional wrestlers, all with an undying passion for the recuperative power of frozen water, in both their ice packs and beer buckets.

Tonight, however, as Otis suddenly saw to his horror, there was more in the freezer than ice cubes and frozen franks. He did a gut-wrenching double-take at the small frosted window in the freezer door, and the hair on his scalp stiffened in a prickly sweat. A human hand, with an ugly red scar in the center of its palm, had wiped a streak of inner frost from the glass and *a benign, bearded face that could belong to no one but Christ himself* was pressed in lifeless rigor against the pane. The glazed, icy-brown eyes seemed to be locked pleadingly on Otis's own as he made a grab for the security interphone.

"Otis?" The sound of his name echoed thinly in the empty hallway. "You okay?"

Otis swallowed hard. "He's dead, Charlie. Christ Almighty, he's *dead!*"

"What? Who's dead?"

"The Messiah, himself," Otis blurted into the mouthpiece, "that's who. He's been iced, Charlie, in more ways than one."

Detective-Lieutenant Cathy Carruthers picked up her telephone on the second ring, with obvious chagrin. Her bedside digital said 5:30 A.M.

"Give me your number," she told the instrument tersely, "and I'll call you back at an earthly hour."

"This is Heller," the telephone responded, "and this is as earthy as it's going to get."

"I said *earthly*, chief, not earthy."

"Whatever -- now listen up, lieutenant, I need you down here on the double. It's PR problem time again, and it's going to take a great deal of finesse and expertise on your part to --"

"On *my* part?"

"Believe you me, lieutenant, you're the only one for the job. This baby's right up your bailiwick."

"But, chief -- *bailiwick*?"

"Glad to see you're with it, lieutenant, so early in the A.M." Captain Henry (Hank) Heller's voice had the cacaphony of half-inch gravel rattling down an empty drainpipe. "The media is on the case already," he rasped, "like a pack of bloody jackals. They're calling it the most heinous crime since Cain slew Abel."

"But, chief --"

"And what was *the* most heinous crime, you ask?"

The lieutenant stifled a yawn. "Okay, so I'm asking. What was *the* --?"

"*That*, lieutenant, is what it's all about. *That*, don't you see, *is* the PR problem, precisely. As a matter of fact, the morning papers have already hit the streets with it, and you wouldn't believe the screamers."

"Try me."

"In three-inch type, no less. I kid you not, lieutenant -- listen, 'MESSIAH DIES MARTYR'S DEATH --'"

"Jesus Christ!"

"Those are your words, lieutenant, not mine. And get this one, 'DIVINE MESSIAH SELF DESTRUCTS --'"
and again, 'MESSIAH CONTRIVES OWN DEMISE --'"

"Hold it, chief, *hold it*. Wait up a minute. You're obviously referring to that professional wrestler, are you not? The one who's been fighting Satan on a nightly basis?"

"Too true, but --"

"Well, then. Don't you think -- uh, in view of the notoriety of the *defunctee*, so to speak, that we could discuss the sordid details of the case just a little later --?"

"Later?" A crescendo of fresh gravel hit the drainpipe. "What's with later?"

"Because, *Mein Kapitan,* at this moment, I am somewhat indisposed."

"You're still in bed?"

"No, I am not in bed, but I *was* in the shower."

"Was?" The gravel made a chuckling sound. "My, my -- when *will* they perfect those new tele-view phones?"

"And when *will* you hang up and let me --"

"Okay, okay. Just get hold of that beach bum you call a partner and meet me down at Lil' Oly's in half an hour. They open at six. I'll fill you in over breakfast, and lieutenant --"

"What now?"

"If you're there on time, I'll spring."

The decisive click of the receiver precluded any further discussion, pro or con. With an indolent shrug of her dripping shoulders, the lieutenant punched out Mark's home number. The phone rang four times before a querulous voice grunted, "Yeah?"

"The chief wants us at Lil' Oly's in half an hour. He's picking up the breakfast tab."

"Half an hour?" Detective-Sergeant Mark Swanson growled his displeasure. "Can't make it. I'm still in the shower."

Cathy Carruthers chuckled. "So was I when the chief called me." Then, after a brief but thoughtful pause, "You've got a telephone in the shower?"

"No, damn it, but I'm shedding water even as I speak, and it's going all over the bloody floor."

The chuckle swelled to a hearty laugh. "We're in parallel plights," she confided, "let's hang up."

"You mean -- well, well, *well.* This has all the happy aspects of an obscene phone call." Mark did some heavy breathing. "Want to go first?"

"Yes. Cool down. Dry off. And get dressed. In that order. And that *is* an order."

"Spoil sport."

"I'll pick you up in twenty minutes."

Mark stalked back to the shower with all the alacrity of a wounded bear. Dressed, Mark Swanson was a big man; naked, he was herculean. His shoulders were mountainous, his abdomen flat and ribbed with muscle. The girth of his compact loins seemed scarcely larger than any one of his massive limbs. As he began again to soap his body, the thought of his comely partner doing the same brought a wistful smile to his handsome, boyish face. He drifted happily away into an X-rated daydream.

Meanwhile, towel in hand, Cathy Carruthers faced her full-length bedroom mirror. She was clearly unaware that a conceptual clone of her naked self *(in the figment of one over-active imagination)* was, at that very moment, cavorting with girlish glee in Mark's steamy shower stall. But no mere mortal, however biased, could hope to justly personify the superb creature that now looked into, and out of, the polished glass.

Her long, lion-like mane seemed to reflect the vibrant colour of ripe wheat; her eyes, the limpid ethereal blue of a summer sky. When she chose to smile, the effect was tantamount to a flash of friendly lightning. Her body was rife in the pulchritude of a Playboy bunny, yet, inexplicably, rippling with the awesome strength and stealth of a jungle cat. She carried her full, firm breasts proudly high, and, when in motion, the musculature in her slender haunches undulated beneath the tawny velvet of her skin with a sensuous mix of womanly grace and raw, predacious power.

She was *The Amazon*, aptly styled by her friends and colleagues in the Homicide Division of Metro Central's Eleventh Precinct. And she was held in deferential awe, as much for her legendary manifestations of almost para-human intelligence, as for the more obvious attributes of her physical presence. No one, other than Mark Swanson, her one true friend and cohort, had ever enjoyed the close personal intimacy vital to even a glimpse of the woman beyond the Amazonian mystique, and then only on regrettably rare occasions. But it was Cathy Carruthers, the woman, undeniably, who toweled dry on this morning of the Divine Messiah's death, and reached for her clothing.

Lil' Oly's was the official unofficial scoff-trough of the Eleventh Precinct. In little more than two years, it had burgeoned under the all but exclusive patronage of the local constabulary; from a sandwich-cum-coffee bar, to cafeteria, to full-fledged restaurant, replete with a *chef de cuisine* (Frenchy, to the boys in blue) and mini-skirted waitresses. It was one of the latter, Mavis, who now approached Captain Hank Heller.

"May I help you, captain, sir?"

Heller's grey eyes flicked impatiently from the waitress's friendly smile to the restaurant's busy entrance, then narrowed keenly as he spotted Cathy Carruthers and Mark Swanson entering through the glass double doors.

"Three coffees, posthaste," Heller told the waitress, "and four breakfast menus. And, Mavis, if you can hold Swanson down to one normal serving of ham 'n' eggs, you'll earn yourself an extra tip."

The girl giggled, then flounced away. By the time she had reappeared with coffee carafe and menus, the two detectives were already seated at the captain's table.

"So," Cathy Carruthers said brightly as she surveyed the restaurant's first thin crop of omnivores, "what's up, chief, apart from your early morning ire?"

Heller scowled at his watch. "I've asked the leprechaun to join us," he said, matching the lieutenant's good cheer with his customary brashness. "He's been putting a file together for the past couple of hours, so we'll wait to hear from him first. In the meantime, we may as well give Mavis our order."

"Great." Mark smiled warmly up at the girl as she waited, pad and pencil in hand. "How're the breakfast steaks this morning, love?"

"Well -- uh --" Mavis looked unduly flustered, torn (Heller speculated) between the promise of monetary gain and a made-to-order opportunity to gladden the eye, and the stomach, of the precinct's most eligible hunk. "Aaah -- not so good, really," she hedged with a sheepish glance at Heller, then, straightening, she bravely added, "but I'm sure I can find a nice one for *you*, sergeant."

Mark rewarded her with a wink (more than she had hoped for) and Heller let his displeasure be known with a surly grunt and a compensatory order of toast and marmalade.

"Make mine the usual," Cathy Carruthers told the girl, "eggnog, if you please, three raw with a touch of nutmeg and -- well, speak of the devil --"

The "devil" who had caught the lieutenant's eye was an elfin little man who was advancing with comic haste toward their table. He carried a huge bundle of files under one little arm while his abbreviated legs seemed to propel him forward in a frenzied kind of whirl, just above floor level.

"He's doing his Jesus walk," Mark noted dryly.

It was, of course, the *leprechaun*, nee Garfield Leprohn, Corporal, the littlest blue-coat this side of Smurfsville (according to Mark) and the incontrovertible *major-domo* of the Records Department. The little man braked to a breathless halt beside the one remaining empty chair, and while his three colleagues looked on in thinly veiled amusement, he proceeded to elevate himself to table-top level with the aid of all but one of the bulky files he had so laboriously carried in. And only then, squinting out from between the ketchup and the cream jug, did he acknowledge the presence of the other three at the table.

The leprechaun wasted no time in formalities. "We've got ourselves a real puzzler this time," he began in a tiny voice befitting his stature. "Murder? Suicide? Accident? Who knows? The only thing I could ascertain for certain, chief, is that a man is dead."

"Yeah, well, Leppy --," Mark took unholy pride in being the little corporal's most devout irritant. "Just give us the facts, eh? We'll do the ascertaining."

The leprechaun bristled. As much as he hated that ignominious epithet, Mark's truncated version of it was even more offensive, aggrandizing one indignity, it seemed, with yet another.

"But the media is calling it suicide," Heller cut in, ignoring Mark's nugacious needling.

"Don't you mean *sacrifice*, chief?" The leprechaun leafed through a well-filled file he had balanced on his little lap. "They (the media) are actually suggesting a comparison, of sorts, between the wrestler's death last night and the historical crucifixion of Christ on the cross. Not in so many works, mind, but most assuredly by implication."

"That's journalism at its yellowest," Cathy Carruthers stated emphatically, "and obviously without the slightest basis in fact. Knowingly, or not, the media are simply aiding and abetting a bunch of money hungry promoters in the perpetuation of what has recently become the most farcical show on earth." She loosed a tremulous sigh. "The *Messiah* versus *Satan* -- yee gods! What next?"

"What is next," the leprechaun asserted, "is that the Messiah (myth or mystic) is undeniably dead. And to the many thousands of rabid devotees of professional wrestling, this means that the second coming, in prophecy and in fact, has come and bloody gone."

"That, Garfield, is somewhat less than funny." The lieutenant's mild rebuke was mollified by her use of his given name, a courtesy he cherished dearly. "You surprise me, really."

The leprechaun dutifully hung his little head.

"I suggest we start by putting this whole mess into some kind of perspective," the lieutenant said to the table at large, then, to the chastened leprechaun in particular, she added, "now suppose you tell us precisely how the man died."

"That's easy, lieutenant, he froze to death in the sports arena's walk-in freezer."

"Did he go into the freezer of his own accord?"

"Apparently so."

"Was he bound, or in any way constrained?"

"No."

"Was he drugged?"

"That, I can't tell you."

"Was the door to the freezer locked?"

"No."

"Then what in heaven's name would deny the man the option of simply walking out?"

"That, lieutenant, if it were on Lil' Oly's menu this morning, would be the *delimme de jour*."

Mavis had hardly begun to serve breakfast when the leprechaun plunked his one working file on the table and began to expound. Dishes were pushed aside to accommodate the rude intrusion.

"As I see it, thus far," the little man said importantly, "there are four principals in the case, including the dead man. Two males and two females, all of whom are wrestlers. A fifth person, the one who discovered the body, is a night watchman called Otis Scroggs. He is not otherwise involved." He paused to take a sip of coffee. "I have a brief history on each of the other four," he added.

"Start with the stiff," Heller told him bluntly.

The leprechaun cleared his tiny throat. "The Messiah, aka The Almighty, or The Prince of Peace, among other tasteless aliases, was born in Oporto, Portugal, in 1945 and has been wrestling for most of his adult life, primarily in Europe. But the name given him at birth was Jesus Podera."

"Jesus Christ!" Mark blurted around a mouthful of medium rare.

"No," the leprechaun countered calmly, "Jesus *Podera*. Podera, by the way, roughly translated from Portugese, means *power.*"

"Jesus Power?" Heller gave a rare grunt of amusement. "With a name like that, who needs Messiah?"

"In Portugal," the lieutenant said in an edifyingly patient voice, "the name, Jesus, is as common as Tom, Dick or Harry on this side of the Atlantic. Still, its religious connotation may have given a certain impetus to the man's somewhat bizarre bent for professional nomenclature."

"Yes, well." The leprechaun coughed softly into a little fist, then went calmly on. "About two years ago, Jesus Podera took up with a lady wrestler and married her. They've been together ever since, working the same circuits. According to the marriage license, her maiden name was, uh -- Mary Mandomski. The name she is currently using in the wrestling ring, however, is Mary Magdalene."

Mark choked into his coffee cup and Heller let out a gutteral whoop that vaguely resembled a burst of laughter. The lieutenant lifted her beautiful eyes heavenward. "That sounds like more of Jesus Podera's obvious proclivity to sacrilege, don't you think?"

The leprechaun was clearly miffed. "It's not my job to moralize, lieutenant, I simply relate the facts as I see them. Now, if you'll permit me to continue --"

"Please do."

The leprechaun please did. "The other male wrestler," he said quietly, "Satan, has also appeared under a multitude of misnomers. The Prince Of Darkness, or Of Devils, or Of Demons -- you name it. But the appellation given him at birth, was --" and here, the little man looked around uneasily" -- Mephisto Schmidt."

"Mephisto!" Mark echoed the name with a howl.

Heller wiped his eyes on his napkin. "Are you sure you've opened the right file, corporal?"

"May I remind you, captain, it's not my job to --"

"Yes, yes, we know. Just the facts, Ma'am. Right? So why don't you give us the name of the other female, corporal? We may as well get this over with."

"Viki Viper," the leprechaun stated flatly, then settled back to weather the predictable outburst. When an element of calm had returned, he carried on.

"Needless to say, Viki Viper is teamed up with Schmidt, and rumour has it that there's been some sort of emotional intrigue brewing between all four of these people."

"One question, corporal." Heller was back to his usual ill-humoured norm. "What makes these three in particular our only suspects in the Messiah's death?"

"Circumstance, captain, nothing more. They were seen with the victim just prior to his death."

"Seen? By whom?"

"By closed-circuit television. The security camera picked up all three wrestlers as they entered the freezer *with* the Messiah."

"Then it must have also picked them up as they all came out without him."

"It did."

"Then the camera would also show if anyone had deliberately locked him in there."

"It would, but it didn't."

"So, to all appearances, Jesus Podera remained inside the freezer entirely of his own accord."

"Yes."

"And you find that premise to be untenable?"

The leprechuan could not suppress a little shiver. "Don't you?"

"Hmmmm. I presume they have all this on tape, corporal."

"They do, sir."

"Then get it."

Heller singled out the lieutenant with a steely stare. "One dead Jesus, a devil's cauldron of Judases, and a videotape of a perfectly normal ice box. What more could you ask for?" He gulped the rest of his coffee and got to his feet. "Like I said, lieutenant, it's right up your bailiwick."

For the lieutenant's ears only, Mark muttered, "Up yours, too, chief."

Heller scrawled his John Henry on Mavis's order pad. "There's a tip in there," he told the girl, "Somewhere between the steak and the eggs. You might try hitting the hunk for the balance."

The Metro Central City Morgue was a low stone structure with long empty echoing halls and quiet tenants. Mark swung the grey unmarked Chevy into a parking slot and killed the motor. He turned to his beautiful partner who graced the seat beside him.

"Don't you think we're a mite early, C.C.?"

"For what?"

"For the autopsy, what else? I doubt if Sam --"

"We haven't come to see Sam, Mark. We've come, you might say, to meet our maker. I want to examine this so-called Messiah before Sam gets at him."

"To what end?"

"To the end of the controversy, I hope. In spite of the chief's colourful prose, Mark, what we have here is one of three distinct scenarios: murder, suicide, or just plain misadventure."

The lieutenant left the car abruptly and Mark followed. He drew abreast of her as they crossed the acre of concrete that prefaced the ornate, heavily-doored entrance. A group of news-people were gathered just inside, clearly visible through the glassed-in front.

"Let's duck that mob, Mark. Sam's got a side entrance just around the corner."

She promptly converted words to action, with Mark hard on her heels. They sped toward a door midway along the side of the building, on which a modest sign was affixed:

SAMUEL MORTON, M.D.
CORONER & CHIEF MEDICAL EXAMINER
M.C.P.D.

The lieutenant tried the door. It was locked. Mark leaned heavily on the bell. A few gesticulating forms appeared around the corner, heading toward them. The door finally inched inward, and the two detectives pushed past a short, dumpy man in a once-white, well-laundered smock that still bore the indelible marks of past mortal migrations under the knife.

"To what," the man snuffed heatedly, "do I owe this outrageous intrusion?"

The lieutenant jerked her golden head toward the open door. "Take a look."

One glimpse of the wildly advancing media types was enough to shift Sam Morton into a Keystone-cop reverse. He slammed, locked, and bolted the heavy door, then stood with his back to it, surveying the two interlopers with mild exacerbation.

"We've got to stop meeting this way," he said with no apparent attempt at humour, "and it's not as though I don't know why you're here."

The lieutenant gave him one of her melting smiles. "Then you'll let us have a look at him?"

"For you, *Wunder Frau*, anything." He met her smile with an endearing leer, then led the way out of his office and down a narrow inner corridor. "I assume you're referring to the Divine One, lieutenant, the guy who came in last night dressed in priestly robes and looking like an iced-lolly."

"The same." She laughed aloud. "Do you treat all your guests so dispassionately, Sam?"

"Only until I get them on the table, my dear." Sam Morton suddenly became Peter Lorre incarnate. "My fondest caress is with my scalpel," he mimed.

The ensuing laughter abruptly fell away as they entered a large tiled room where the cryptic chill of death seemed to burden the very air they breathed. The room's one occupant reclined somberly beneath a sheet that had been noticeably subjected to as many fruitless ablutions as the M.E.'s smock.

"You haven't begun the autopsy then," Mark noted hopefully.

"Are you kidding, Mark? Remember how long it took to thaw out your last Christmas turkey?"

Mark and the lieutenant exchanged ashen glances.

"Well, add to that the complicacies of rigor mortis and you'll get some idea of what we're up against. That's why he's in here, to hurry up the process."

"Why the rush?"

"What Heller wants, Heller gets," the M.E. stated flatly, "come Hell-er high water." He chuckled at his own quip, then added, "Sometimes."

"Have you examined him, Sam?"

"Only perfunctorily, lieutenant."

"Did you happen to notice any epidermal signs of possible drugging?"

"No."

"What about external marks of restraint?"

The dumpy coroner shrugged his shoulders. "He was not bound when he arrived here, but, let's take a look." He drew aside the soiled shroud.

The two detective's were visibly startled at the indisputable likeness of the dead man's countenance to the graphic depictions of Christ as portrayed by the Renaissance masters. The facial hair, the high cheek bones, the sensuous mouth; every detail appeared to be meticulously replicated from a fourteenth century canvas. Even the long white flowing robes he wore were indicative of that period in time when the Gallilean walked the earth.

"Look at his hands," Mark said with a note of awe.

Both palms bore the scars of what might have been the running through of spikes. The feet, too, just below each ankle, had similar wounds. There were no detectable signs of rope burns.

"Plastic surgery," Sam Morton said without hesitation, "the nail scars, I mean. Quite obvious, in fact, to a medically trained eye."

"And spurious," the lieutenant added. "Those who were unfortunate enough to be crucified by nailing (some were tied), the nails, of necessity, had to be driven through *above* the wrists, in order to support the weight of the body. Let's look at his side."

The M.E. bared the man's right torso. A long ugly red scar marred the otherwise unblemished flesh.

"The man was an unconscionable charlatan. He has obviously gone to preposterous lengths to fabricate a macabre and tasteless hoax." The lieutenant turned and headed for the door. "I've seen enough."

Their eyes met over their coffee cups as they sat across from each other at a small table outside Luigi's, a side-walk cafe half a block from Metro Central's Memorial Arena. It was lunch time.

"So what's on the agenda, beautiful?"

Cathy Carruthers treated her favorite tellurian to a flash of friendly lightning. "What do you say to some *t'ai chi chu'an?*"

Mark beamed. "Chinese food? Great. Your place or mine?"

"*T'ai chi chu'an*, Mark, is a form of Chinese wrestling."

"Better still. Your place or mine?"

The lieutenant laughed. "Why don't we settle for the Arena? It's less than a block away. I'd like to get better acquainted with those two lady grapplers, Viki Viper and Mary Magdalene -- not to mention the notorious Herr Mephisto Schmidt."

"Well, each to his own proclivity," Mark muttered ruefully. "After our last encounter with a wrestler, I just hope these three weirdos are still alive."

"And talkative."

There were half a dozen men lazing about the ring, large men, in a motley array of casual attire, save one, and he stood out from the others like a leper at a love-in. He was dressed in black; black hood, black cape, black leotards, black body-shirt, black boots and gloves. Even his face was a congenital black. The only relief from that ominous hue was a pair of red horns jutting from his hood and a red pitchfork emblazoned across his enormous chest. He was, without question, Herr Satan.

The ring was lit, and two women in abbreviated tights and tops, were listlessly rehearsing a variety of wrestling moves. One was heavy-thighed, thick-waisted and busty; the other, lithe and shapely, almost pretty, with an obviously concocted air of chasteness about her that made her look more vulnerable than she deserved beside her beefy opponent. It was not difficult to distinguish between Mary Magdalene and her arch foe, Viki Viper.

The approach of Cathy Carruthers and Mark Swanson went unnoticed, until they came in under the canopy of light that illuminated the ring. The Satanic one was the first to spot them.

"Vell, vell," he intoned gutturally, "vas dis?"

"Are you Mephisto Schmidt?" the lieutenant asked quietly.

"And who vants to know?"

"Just answer the question, clown," Mark told the man with steely evenness.

The big German black was not accustomed to being told to do anything by anyone, much less be called a clown. He locked his dark eyes firmly onto Mark's, looking for an edge, a sign of weakness. The huge arena had become as silent as a tomb.

"Answer the question," Mark said again.

"I am Mephisto Schmidt," the big black snarled, "who the hell are you?"

The lieutenant flashed her badge and went through the routine of introduction.

Schmidt ignored her. "No one calls Schmidt a clown," he said to Mark.

"I just did," Mark asserted softly.

For a big man, Schmidt moved swiftly. He lunged at Mark with a squawk of anger, his big paws clutching wildly at thin air as Mark stepped adroitly to one side. Then, before the enraged wrestler could regain his balance, a fist the size of a leg-o'-mutton slammed squarely against the point of the big black's jaw. Satan dropped to his knees like a repentant sinner.

Mary Magdalene let out a squeal from the centre of the ring. With practiced opportunism, she spied an unsuspecting Cathy Carruthers standing a scant two feet from the ring's edge. She leapt like a rabbit, grabbing two handfuls of golden hair and with the aid of the ropes, she hoisted the startled detective up into a loping jackknife. A cheer went up from the ringside wrestlers as the lieutenant landed in a tangle of limbs and disheveled clothing in the middle of the canvas, her head nodding dizzily.

"Go get her, Mary."

"She's a doozer."

"Yeah, get some of them clothes off her."

"If you don't," someone bellowed, "Viki bloody will."

There was a chorus of laughter as Viki Viper took the bait, moving in to join the fray.

Mark jumped to the apron. He was about to duck under the ropes when strong hands grabbed at his legs. He looked back to see five large men holding his feet firmly to the canvas. Satan was still well out of it.

Then a sudden spate of activity drew his eyes back to the ring. And Mark knew, as he saw the veil of vertigo leave her eyes, that it was no longer Cathy Carruthers out there, skirt and blouse, half on, half off, flipping suddenly to her feet as though propelled by a steel spring and tossing her would-be assailants aside like a couple of rag dolls.

It was *The Amazon*, tall and proud, front and centre. One in each hand, by the scruff of their necks, she lifted the two stunned lady wrestlers three feet off the canvas floor and brought their heads together with a resounding *thwack*! that could be heard in the most distant reaches of the arena. They fell senseless, in a convoluted heap at her feet. Then, with lightning speed and precision, the Amazon levelled her superb body in a blistering dropkick, squarely at the heads of two of the wrestlers still clinging to her chosen cohort. The hapless pair sagged back and down to join Satan on the concrete floor.

Mark then diminished the odds further still by pistoning the heel of one freed foot into the already cauliflowered visage of one more witless grappler. All that remained now was a little mopping up, which the Amazon left in Mark's capable hands (and fists) while she went about retrieving her dissimulated ensemble. With a nip here and a tuck there, plus a few minor adjustments, she resurfaced, moments later, as a slightly soiled but highly present-able, Cathy Carrutherds.

"You were great," Mark told her as he nursed the knuckles of his right hand.

"I can handle myself when I have to," she replied indifferently.

"Yeah," Mark grinned, "that, too."

Uniformed police arrived soon after the scuffle had ended, at the behest of Arena Security (who had seen the entire incident on closed-circuit television). They were gathering up the addled behemoths to cart them off to the pokey when the lieutenant addressed one of the uniforms.

"Hold the two women for questioning, officer, and that guy in the devil's outfit. As for the rest, just hang onto them until they've seen the light."

"Yes, ma'am." The officer's eyes were saucers of wonder-ment. "But by the look of them, lieutenant, that might be a while."

"And he ain't just whistling Dixie," a deep, throaty voice said behind her. She turned to face a large, rumpled-looking man whom she guessed to be in his late sixties. He was bald and noticeably bereft of all facial hair. He reminded her of Telly Savalas, without eyebrows.

"I'm Garth Gibson," he said, proffering a large hairless hand, "also known as the Albino Assassin." He laughed good-naturedly. "But that was back in my misspent youth. Today, I run this joint. I'm the current promoter of Central City Wrestling."

The lieutenant took his hand. "What can I do for you?"

"It's not what you can do for me, lieutenant, it's what I can do for you."

"Oh?"

"I saw the whole donnybrook on Security TV," he said with unbridled enthusiasm, "and, well -- I was impressed."

"Were you, now?"

"No, no. Don't get me wrong, lieutenant. I'm not talking cheap thrills here." His pinky-looking eyes were painfully apologetic. "I'm willing to offer you, and that guy you're with, one million dollars, lieutenant, for twelve months work. God's truth. Of course," he said apprehensively, "he'd have to quit using those bloody great fists of his. We all want to survive, you know."

The lieutenant heard Mark's playful chuckle at her elbow. "Did you hear that?" she asked him.

"Faith, and I did at that," he responded in his best Irish accent, "but I'd be warnin' yu, sir. I'll not be settlin' fur nuthin' less then top billin'."

The already bemused promoter looked suddenly stunned. "You mean --"

"The man, himself, begorra." Mark was doing what he could to look godly and serious at one and the same time. "Now, I ask yu," he spoofed, "how else yu goin' t'be teachin' the likes of that black divil to toe the line?"

When the shenanigans were over, and the pallid promoter had given up all hope of recruiting new talent from the M.C.P.D., he proved to be a veritable well-spring of information.

"Oh, yeah, the Messiah was good," he told Mark and the lieutenant over a cup of coffee in his office, "that guy's probably drawing crowds right now, in heaven -- or wherever the hell he went to." He laughed at his own inept humour. "He had this hold, see? He called it the 'laying on of hands.' Can you believe it? He'd grab a guy by his graps (that's the *trapezius* muscle, between the neck and the shoulder), and he would squeeze on some nerve, or something. And, well -- that'd be all she wrote, lieutenant. Manana."

"Come o-o-on." Mark was unimpressed. "A so-called submission hold? I've seen them all. And they are all as phoney as a tit in a tantrum."

"Mark!" The lieutenant gave him an elbow.

"Not this one," Gibson insisted. "In fact, that's where the trouble all began. The other guys were willing to fake it. For self preservation, if nothing else. But Jesus came on with this bolt-of-lightning bit like he was God Almighty, himself."

"So he wasn't particularly liked."

"Lieutenant, he was *hated*. Anyone of dozens of men would have gladly pulled his plug."

"What about the girls?"

"Well, it don't take much savvy to see that Viki Viper is on an AC/DC circuit. Both she and Mephisto had the same diddly itch for little Mary."

"But Jesus was in the way?"

"You got it right, lieutenant, *was* in the way."

"Mmmm." The lieutenant grew quietly pensive. "We seem to have ample motive, as well as ample opportunity. And while we still can't prove the Messiah's death to be anything other than misadventure, the circumstances surrounding his demise are so bizarre, we simply must *assume* he was in some way coerced into remaining inside that freezer after the other three had left."

"How long was it before they discovered the body?" Mark asked.

"Just shy of four A.M.," Gibson stated firmly. "I happen to know because they got me out of bloody bed when they found him."

"Yeah, but how long was he in there?"

"A good three hours."

"And he was frozen solid?" The lieutenant looked perplexed. "That hardly seems long enough to --"

"Aaah," Gibson broke in, "a good point, lieutenant. Under normal functioning, the inside freezer temperature would be about

-10 Celsius, which is pretty damn cold and may well have done the job in any case. However, when the Messiah's body was found early this morning, the temperature in the freezer had dropped to almost -25. Someone had tampered with the thermostat."

"But if the temperature in the freezer is controllable, why couldn't the Messiah have simply turned it down? Or off, for that matter?"

"The thermostat, lieutenant, is mounted on the outer wall."

"Outside the door?"

"Yes."

"In view of the security camera?"

"Yes."

"Well, now we're getting somewhere. Anyone tampering with the thermostat would have been seen by the camera, right?"

"I would think so."

"Then it's time we took a look at that videotape." The lieutenant got to her feet, then hesitated. "Mr. Gibson," she said, "before we leave the Arena, do you think you could join us in a brief visit to the scene of the deed, as it were?"

"Don't you mean the scene of the *dead,* as it *is*?" the promoter replied with a crusty chuckle. "Either way, lieutenant, it'd be a pleasure."

The hall was four feet wide and approximately fifty feet long. They came into it as Otis Scroggs had done, from behind the concession stand. Midway down the hall, on their right, the security interphone rested in a small niche, directly across from the walk-in freezer.

"This, then, is the thermostat," the lieutenant observed, as she pointed to a plastic wall-mounted dial, about two feet from the heavy casing of the freezer door. She looked up to locate the camera, which hung suspended from the ceiling at the far end of the hall. "Anyone touching that thermostat," she mused aloud, "could not possibly escape the eye of the camera."

"But why," Mark queried, "would anyone deliberately incriminate themselves in front of a camera? They must have known it was there."

The lieutenant shrugged her impeccable eyebrows. "Why indeed?"

"But it was tampered with," the promoter insisted, "the camera must have picked up *something.*"

"We'll soon see," the lieutenant said idly, her attention now drawn to the handle on the freezer door. It was a one-sided pull-type lever, hinged inside a sturdy metal housing. She tugged the door slightly ajar, then closed it again. When in the closed position, she noticed, a small oblong gap was exposed at the butt end of the handle, large enough to accommodate two of her well-manicured fingers. She tried opening the door with her fingers still in the gap and found she could not. But most surprising, was the lack of any meaningful pressure on her fingers as she tugged on the handle.

"The mechanism in this thing is certainly well engineered," she said as she opened the door again and went inside. The icy chill of the freezer enveloped her at once and her breath came out in misty puffs. The room was about twenty feet by ten, the walls lined with shelves of frozen foods. A huge ice-cube unit dominated the far wall. As she turned to leave, the lieutenant saw that simple egress was ensured by pushing on a round, dish-like handle which responed to the slightest pressure.

"Mark," she called around the door's edge, "when I close the door, put your finger in that gap at the butt end of the handle." She re-entered the freezer, and with Mark's big finger in place, she tried again to open the door. This time, it remained closed, and no amount of pushing on the handle would budge it. She signalled him through the small glass window to let her out.

"It seems clear enough," she said as she joined the men in the hall, "that any object, about an inch and a quarter long, by maybe three-quarters wide, and deep, if placed in that gap, would prevent the door from being opened, from either side."

"There was nothing in there when they found the body," Gibson reminded her. "The guys from security just walked right in and pulled him out."

"Of course, it could have been removed."

Gibson gave a raspy laugh. "You're back to the camera again, lieutenant."

"Right." The lieutenant dropped to one knee and sighted along an imaginary line from the door to the camera. "If some foreign object was inserted in the door handle, and subsequently removed, the camera would, indeed, have seen it. Come on, Mark, let's go to the movies."

The leprechaun was ready and waiting as the lieutenant and Mark entered the Eleventh Precinct's dimly-lit projection room. A lone policewoman sat in one of the leather seats with her eyes glued to the television screen.

"Thank God you're finally here," she said wearily, "Nothing has moved up there for almost three hours."

The TV screen showed the camera's-eye-view of the empty hall in the Arena where the two detectives had parted company with promoter Garth Gibson less than an hour before.

"I had to have someone monitor the screen," the leprechaun explained from the shadows behind them, "from the time the wrestlers left the freezer until the watchman, Otis Scroggs, finally found the body. Scroggs, by the way, is due to appear any minute now."

"Fisk," the lieutenant said, addressing the pretty brunette rookie, "are you saying that no one has entered that hall since the wrestlers left?"

"Not a soul, lieutenant. Four wrestlers went into the freezer, three came out. That's it."

"And nothing since?"

"Nothing."

"Here's Scroggs," the leprechaun said suddenly.

They all looked on as the night watchman acted out his traumatic discovery of the Messiah through the window in the freezer door, along with his subsequent call to Security. Then, in a matter of minutes, another guard appeared, and together they opened the freezer door and dragged out the dead Messiah. At that point, Scroggs left, only to reappear seconds later with a blanket to cover the body.

"They sure as hell didn't have any trouble opening the door," Mark noted.

"Tell me about it," the lieutenant said with a heavy sigh, "so there goes the convenient foreign-object-in-the-handle theory." She turned to the leprechaun. "Run it back, Garfield, to when the wrestlers first appear. Maybe this time we'll get lucky."

The videotape took some time to rewind and the lieutenant used the interlude to further solicit from Officer Fisk her absolute assurance that nothing had moved in the empty hall during her long vigil. The young woman was unshakeable.

"My eyes never left the screen," she stated emphatically. "I'd have seen a fly move, had there been one."

"I'm more interested," the lieutenant told her, "in insights, than insects."

"Ready when you are," the leprechaun announced with as much felicitous flair as he could muster.

The lieutenant waited patiently while Mark fired up a coffin nail. "One dead; one dying," she said with a sigh of mild reproof, then, "Okay, Garfield, roll it."

The screen lit up with the same view of the empty hall.

"There's a lead time here of about two minutes," the little man told them. "Prior to this shot, there was traffic in and out of the freezer from both wrestlers and staff, but nothing out of the ordinary."

There was another minute of empty silence before the screen came alive. The four wrestlers could then be seen approaching the freezer in a tight group, their backs to the camera. The Messiah was first, then Mary Magdalene, with Viki Viper close behind. Herr Satan brought up the rear, carrying an empty ice bucket, while his broad back was managing to eclipse a clear view of the other three. But even then, as they passed the thermostat, there was an almost imperceptible flicker of movement between Satan's back and the wall.

"Hold it," the lieutenant said quickly, "run that back a bit."

The leprechaun deftly followed instructions. Then, with the

tape rolling again, and on the lieutenant's sudden cry of "*There!*" the wrestlers all froze in mid-stride. The blurred image of a white hand had made contact with the dial of the thermostat. It was impossible to tell to whom the hand belonged.

"That," the lieutenant asserted quietly, "is the hand of the murderer. But whose hand is it?"

"It sure as hell isn't Satan's," Mark said with certainty, "wrong colour."

"And one would hardly expect the Messiah to assist in his own demise," the lieutenant added.

"Which," the brown-eyed Fisk chimed in brightly, "only leaves the two women."

"Good thinking," the lieutenant said with an amused chuckle. "Can this scene be blown up, corporal?"

"Yes, there is a process. But it will take some time."

"Get it. And do you see that tiny glint of light on one of the fingers? That's what I'm after. Okay, let's see the rest of it."

The wrestlers sprang to life again, only to disappear one at a time, into the freezer. After about a minute, the door opened and Satan re-emerged, his bucket, now filled to overflowing with ice cubes, in one hammy fist. He was out of the picture in seconds. Viki Viper came out next, closely followed by Mary Magdalene. Both women were empty handed as they closed the door behind them and moved off slowly toward the camera.

"Hold it, corporal."

The tape stopped on the lieutenant's command. "Roll that back a little, to just before the door closes. That's it. Now, let it come -- slowly --"

There was no sound in the projection room as all eyes focussed on Mary Magdalene, the last one to leave the freezer. They saw her slowly, gently, ease the door shut, then, as she walked away from it, her hand trailed lightly, almost casually, along the lever-like handle, until it finally dropped away.

"Nothing there," Mark said as the two women moved out of camera range.

"Agreed," Fisk piped up, happy this time to have an ally.

"To be frank, lieutenant," the leprechaun said tentatively, "I, too, saw nothing."

"Get a blow-up of Mary Magdalene's hand on the door handle, corporal." The lieutenant rose lightly to her feet. "No rush. But it would be nice to wrap this case up, sometime tomorrow."

"Wrap it up?"

"There are always loose ends at the conclusion of every case. You know that, Garfield." She turned to Mark. "How about some *sushi*, and a bottle of dry wine?"

"Does this mean what I think it does?" Mark asked cautiously. "You now know who done what to who?"

"To *whom*, Mark, and I'll ignore the rest of the sentence. But, yes, I do know. Now all we have to do is prove it. So, what about that *sushi*?"

Mark wondered if he would ever be able to take his partner's sudden augeries in stride. He decided to capitulate. "Your place or mine?" he sighed.

"Mine." Cathy Carruthers flashed one of her irridescent smiles. "I feel safer on familiar territory."

Lieutenant Cathy Carruthers sat side-saddle on one of the many desks in the Eleventh Precinct's spacious squad room. Mark Swanson, as could be expected, was close at her elbow. The three disgruntled wrestlers, Schmidt, Magdalene and Viper, had been given chairs on the low, room-wide dais in front of the desks.

"So vat's dis about?" the Satanic menace wanted to know.

"Yeah," Viki Viper muttered, looking dumpy and mannish in a loose-fitting sweater and slacks.

"Yeah," echoed a mini-skirted Mary Magdalene, her ring-wise aura of innocent vulnerability having seemingly evaporated overnight.

"All in due time --" the lieutenant began, then turned abruptly, as chief Hank Heller came bursting into the room like an early morning sand storm.

"Don't have much time, lieutenant," he rasped, "let's get this over with."

"We're waiting for the leprechaun," she told him calmly.

"Again?"

"Again." The lieutenant glanced impatiently toward the door. "And here he is."

The leprechaun did not exactly burst into the room as his chief had done; he sort of popped in, like a pea out of a pea-shooter, with his usual bulky bundle of files tucked securely under one little arm. He dumped himself into a chair behind one of the desks and promptly disappeared from view, an embarrassment he was quick to rectify, with the help of a goodly portion of his documental burden.

The little corporal's colleagues politely refrained from any outward display of amusement, but the somewhat less-than-saintly Mary Magdalene was not so gracious. "A midget wrestler," she giggled. "Oh, I love the little darling. --"

"Did you bring the blow-ups, corporal?" the lieutenant cut in quickly, hoping to defuse a visibly irate leprechaun, who, at that moment, looked to be on the verge of blowing up, himself. The little man rummaged in his reams of data to produce not two, but several large photographs. He then basked openly in the lieutenant's commendatory smile as she took them from him.

"I see you've second guessed me, Garfield," she said as she scanned the enlargements. "Good work. Good work, indeed."

The lieutenant then ascended the dais to stand before the three wrestlers. "May I see a show of hands, please?"

The three grapplers looked confused, then, one by one, with some reluctance, they held their hands out in front of them. The lieutenant singled out Mary Magdalene, on whose left hand, alone, a thin platinum ring reposed.

"Would you agree, Mary," the lieutenant asked as she thrust one of the enlargements under the woman's nose, "that this is your hand?"

Mary Magdalene glanced sidelong at the photograph and shrugged her shoulders. "How would I know?"

"It has your ring on it."

"So what?"

"Only this, dear lady. That hand belongs not only to you; it is also the hand of the person who murdered Jesus Podera."

There was an audible hush in the room. The accused wrestler looked open-eyed from Viki Viper to Mephisto Schmidt, then back to the lieutenant. She was openly distraught.

Schmidt spoke first. "Don't let her scare you, Mary. Jesus' death was an accident. That picture don't prove nothin'."

"No, it doesn't," the lieutenant agreed, "not in itself, but rest assured, we have more to go on than that. Nor am I suggesting, Mr. Schmidt, that you and Viki Viper are in any way blameless in the Messiah's murder. But first, Mary, let me pose a scenario, a sequence of events, if you like, of what really happened last night, prior to the discovery of Jesus Podera's frozen body."

The lieutenant seemed to grow in stature as she paced, slowly, back and forth behind the three detainees. Their eyes followed her warily as she moved into, and out of, their peripheral vision. Mary Magdalene, in particular, was visibly shaken.

"As I see it," the lieutenant began, "it had already been decided among you, for whatever reason, that Mary Magdalene would be the one to reach out and trip the thermostat on your collective way to the freezer, amply concealed (so you thought) from the camera's view, not just by huddling together, as you did, but by the broad back of Mephisto Schmidt. However, as this enlargement testifies, that part of your nefarious scheme has clearly failed."

The lieutenant paused to draw an errant tress of flaxen hair from her forehead with an elegantly arched middle finger. The silence in the room was profound.

"How you persuaded an unsuspecting Jesus Podera to lead the way into the freezer," she continued, "and then linger there, while the rest of you made a hasty exit, we may never know. Still, I seriously doubt that a simple deceit of this nature would present much of a problem. But then, and again according to plan, once the Messiah was left alone in the freezer, it fell to Mary Magdalene, with those same cunningly manipulative hands of hers, to keep him there." She confronted the lady wrestler directly. "And that, Mary, is precisely what you did. We have it all on tape."

Mary Magdalene was on the quiet side of panic. "What've you got on tape?" Her voice was susurrus hiss. "What've you got on tape, lieutenant?"

"Take a look." The lieutenant spread the enlargements and held them up in front of her. "They show you doing it."

"Doing *what*, for chrissake?" She struck the prints from the lieutenant's hands. They fluttered to the floor where Mark and Heller promptly retrieved them. The leprechaun was smiling smugly.

"Some small object," the lieutenant told the room at large, "had to be inserted into that gap at the butt end of the outer handle, to prevent the man inside the freezer from opening the door and escaping. There was no other way to keep him in there. But that 'object' had to be something that would not later have to be retrieved in full view of the camera."

Mary Magdalene was on her feet. "Bullshit!" she screamed. "You ain't pinning this rap on me."

"Shut up," Schmidt snarled. He tried to tug her back down into the chair. "Just *shut up!*"

"*You* shut up, you Nazi bastard. I ain't taking no fall for you. And I ain't taking no fall for that quirky queen of yours, neither. You were the ones who set this all up in the first place."

Schmidt and Viper rolled their eyes in unison as they sagged back in their chairs. The lieutenant moved in quickly.

"Are you prepared to make a statement to that effect, Mary?"

"Yeah, sure. Why not?" She gave a grotesque little giggle of defeat. "I know when I'm licked, even if they don't." She shook her head ruefully. "But you've got to give the devil his due, lieutenant, Mephisto had it figured out pretty good."

"But not good enough," was the lieutenant's grim response.

Mary Magdalene sat at one of the desks in the squad room, laboriously reading through a statement that had been drawn up in preparation for her signature. On the other side of the room, the lieutenant, Mark and Heller were gathered around the leprechaun who was still propped up on his pile of data like a toddler waiting for his first haircut.

Mark was shuffling through the enlargements. "You know, C.C., these things don't really show anything substantial at all." He kept his voice low, out of reach of the lady wrestler. "Some of them are just a bloody blur. I doubt a magistrate would even accept --"

"Not the point, Mark," the lieutenant told him softly. "Mary Magdalene accepted them, and that's what counts."

"But she hardly glanced at them."

The lieutenant chuckled. "Maybe that's why. But let's not forget, Mark, that she *is* guilty, by her own admission, and is willing to confess to it. How she arrived at that decision is immaterial."

"What I want to know," Heller barked under his breath, "is how they got the guy to stay inside that freezer while all the rest of them were getting the hell out, lickety-split?"

"The way Magdalene tells it," the lieutenant reflected, "was that she had intentionally 'forgotten' to bring along their ice bucket, hers and Jesus', and on the pretext of going back to get it, she obligingly left him there to wait for her return. He had no reason, then, to think that she would not. The videotape bears her out, if you recall, which shows only Mephisto Schmidt carrying an empty bucket into the freezer."

"No, I don't recall it, lieutenant, but I'll take your word for it. Now what about the 'foreign object' bit? How was it done? Locking him in there, I mean."

"Ingenious, but simple, as all ingenious things are," the lieutenant recounted, "a common ice cube, chief, in the dexterous hand of Mary Magdalene was surreptitiously dropped into the gap at the butt end of the handle as she left the freezer. By the time the body was found, the ice cube had melted, restoring unobstructed access to the freezer. The small residual melt from the ice cube had either dried up by then, or gone unnoticed."

"So all this BS about blow-ups," Mark said in a disparaging undertone, "was just so much hog wash." He grinned at the little man on his stack of papers. "You might even say that the whole effort fell a little short."

The leprechaun blinked and blushed as only he could. But he kept his cool. The knowing smirk he had donned when the lieutenant had first taken the prints from him, was still implacably in place.

"Not entirely, Mark." The lieutenant treated the leprechaun to a reassuring smile. "As blurred and as indistinct as some of the prints were, they did serve to corroborate a rather tenuous theory. The first print, to be precise, exposed the ring on Magdalene's finger as it touched the thermostat. So far, so good. The second and third prints revealed what might reasonably be construed as the ice cube being skillfully dropped into place in the handle. A bit thin, but credible. But the last three or four, which were taken from the tape some time after the wrestlers had left --"

"One hour later, lieutenant," the leprechaun proudly interjected, "precisely."

"Yes, well, what they showed (and clearly this time) was a minute flow of water, trickling from the handle as the ice cube melted. That clinched it."

"And the motive?" Mark was eager to change the subject.

"Well, as the promoter, Garth Gibson, emphatically informed us earlier, Mark, Jesus Podera was hated by all and sundry. The needless cruelty he apparently inflicted on the other wrestlers in the ring, he carried over into his private life. He must have put his wife (if you'll pardon a bad pun) through hell. And although it was actually Mephisto Schmidt who planned the murder, he found in Mary Magdalene, a willing, if not eager, accomplice."

"Lieutenant?" Mary Magdalene was timidly approaching the small group still gathered around the leprechaun.

"Yes?"

The woman looked painfully disspirited. "It says here," she said, tracing her finger along a line in the prepared statement, "that Mephisto and Viki were, uh -- 'accessories, *after* the fact,' and that it was me, lieutenant, who really killed Jesus."

"Well?"

"But it was *him*, lieutenant, Mephisto. I wouldn't have done nothing if it hadn't been for him. He *made* me do it, lieutenant, him and Viki." She was on the verge of tears. "I think that should be in here, lieutenant."

"Fair enough, Mary. We'll type in an addendum to that effect." The lieutenant took the statement from the woman and handed it directly to the leprechaun. "Did you get that, corporal?"

The leprechaun looked momentarily at a loss. "What should I say?"

"What else?" Cathy Carruthers could not suppress a wide mischievous grin. "Just say, '*The devil made me do it*'."

Sara Plews

Sara Plews' first published short story, "The Maltise Salami". Like famous falcon, it disappeared many years ago. Her second story, "Murder by the Tubful", appeared in Peter Sellers' first Mosaic Press anthology, *COLD BLOOD: Murder in Canada*. Like that tale, "Good Night, Mrs. Calabash, Wherever You Are" is another complex and compact puzzler.

GOODNIGHT, MRS. CALABASH, WHEREVER YOU ARE

by Sara Plews

So the light was green and Quinn stepped off the curb and this guy got out of a blue Buick and shot him.

Quinn wasn't surprised. Pedestrians are never surprised.

"Hey, fella, you all right?"

The little guy in the black horn-rimmed glasses peered down at Quinn.

"You don't look so good."

Quinn didn't feel so good, either. It occurred to him that he had never spent so much time in the gutter.

The little guy heard Quinn's giggle, but what he said was: "Say, that's a mighty nice briefcase you got there. Hey, I'll just hang on to it 'til we know what, okay?"

Quinn watched the little guy walk away. He wanted to shout something, but the Cabbage Patch clouds were so cute.

"Listen, don't suppose ya can move, huh?"

Quinn watched this cucumber nose stuck in a potato face point accusingly at him.

"I mean, Christ, of all the cabs ya hadda fall in front of. I told the old bag I'd be home by five, ya know. She thinks I'm bagging this new dispatcher. I mean, I am, but I promised the bitch I'd be home by five. Listen, maybe if I give you a hand, we can get ya on the sidewalk."

The cucumber nose was serious, Quinn could see that. He wondered what he should do, then forgot what he was supposed to be wondering about. The only thing he could think of was the sandbox. Hell, it was more than 25 years ago. He was in this sandbox, with those little soldiers that used to be in the cornflakes. His sister wanted to play, he said no; she asked again, he said no; she asked again, he hit her in the mouth. In that split second before the shriek, he watched as a fat teardrop readied itself for its slide down a pudgy cheek.

Quinn began to cry.

*   *   *   *   *

The first time he opened his eyes, he wished he hadn't. Death, he was sure, was a lot less painful.

The second time, he saw the doctor.

"You'll live," he was told.

Quinn wanted to whine: his chest was too tight, the tube in his nose and the tube in his side were a pain in the ass, he had to go to the bathroom.

But, when he opened his mouth, he noticed the doctor wasn't there. He stared at the ceiling, instead.

*   *   *   *   *

The red-nosed cop picked up the rice pudding from Quinn's tray and stared at it.

"Hey, listen Quinn, ya don't wanna talk, don't worry. Best thing, ya know, get better, back on your feet, we'll talk then, okay? I mean, ya coulda been dead, right?"

The cop continued to stare at the rice pudding.

"I don't suppose ya wanna tell me about the money, huh?"

Quinn looked at him.

The cop laughed. "Hadda try, right?"

He stared at the pudding one last time, shook his head, then dumped it into the can beside the bed.

Quinn closed his eyes and listened to the footsteps fade out the door.

*   *   *   *   *

It happened about an hour after the rubber chicken. Quinn smelled the perfume first. He was in the chair, facing the window, watching the rain. The perfume was behind Quinn, then to his side. He turned and looked up.

"Hello, Quinn," she said.

He nodded, then turned back to the window and the rain.

"I'm sorry," she said, and bent down. Her warm breath near his ear still did funny things to him. Her lips brushed his cheek.

Quinn continued to watch the raindrops beading on the window. He heard her settle on the edge of the bed. He wanted to turn to her, to reach out, to take her in his arms, to kiss her, to run his hands over her hair, to slip them around her soft tanned neck, to squeeze, to watch her yellow eyes bulge...

Instead, he said: "How did Frank find out?"

He heard her take a deep breath.

"I ... I told him, Quinn. I had to."

Quinn laughed.

"Listen, dammit, he knew there was someone. You know what he's like. He would've killed me."

Quinn shook his head.

"Face it, kiddo, you wanted the money for yourself. Too bad about your timing, though."

Quinn heard her get off the bed. She came between him and the window and the rain.

"What do you mean?"

Quinn looked up at her.

"Guess what I was carrying when Frankie came ashootin'?"

Her eyes widened.

"You idiot! You were supposed to leave the money --"

"Ya, like I can trust you, right?"

She sighed.

"All right, Quinn, tell me where the money's at. Maybe I can keep Frank off your back."

Quinn laughed, but his chest hurt, so he stopped.

"Quinn, for God's sake, where is it?"

He didn't say anything for a while.

She went back to the bed, picked up her raincoat, shrugged into it.

He waited until he knew she was at the door.

"Tell him Crazy Aldo," he said without turning.

"What?" she said.

"Crazy Aldo. Tell Frank it's Crazy Aldo."

Long after she left him, he was still staring at the window and the rain.

*   *   *   *   *

Quinn knew it was time to leave the hospital when Crazy Aldo made the papers. He had been staring at the Page 3 girl ("Stella likes hang-gliding and eighteenth century German literature") when a boxed item to the right of the leopard-skin-encased bum caught his eye.

ALDO NO MORO

The body of a small-time crook was found last night in a parking lot beside the downtown Spadina Hotel, Metro Toronto Police say.

Aldo (Crazy Aldo) Moro, 47, of Dovercourt Rd., was apparently beaten to death, homicide Staff-Sergeant Dave Bandert said. An empty battered briefcase was next to the body, he said.

The hotel's night bartender discovered the body when he tripped over it, Bandert said.

Moro's record, which included convictions for theft, breaking and entering, illegal possession, fraud and forgery, stretched back to the 1950s.

Bandert said Moro was dubbed Crazy Aldo in the summer of 1966 when he apparently knocked over a motorcycle belonging to the leader of the Black Diamonds. Six policemen and 15 bikers were injured in the ensuing Lessard Park riot.

*   *   *   *   *

The first thing Quinn did was check his mailbox in the lobby of his apartment building. When he saw the card from the post office, he smiled. He liked it when a plan came together.

On Queen Street, he went into a bargain-basement electronics store. The bullet-headed owner separated his cigar from his lips long enough to grunt at Quinn. Then he yelled at a callow youth: "Hey, Ralph, ya jerk, watch the store a sec, huh?"

He led Quinn into a back room and took down a briefcase from one of the shelves. He showed Quinn how to open it, then gave him the case.

On the sidewalk outside the store, Quinn groaned. Frank just laughed.

"Hey, buddy, can ya spare a briefcase?"

Quinn saw the blue Buick at the curb, a suited thug behind the wheel. He smelled the perfume before he realized she was there, too.

"I'm sorry," she said, treating Quinn to her favourite line.

Frank laughed again. He took the briefcase from Quinn.

"Listen, buddy, me an' you gonna have us some fun. Well, maybe jus' me. I'll bet ya you're gonna jus' die thinkin' 'bout when you're gonna get it."

He moved away from Quinn, toward the car.

"Don't get in the car," Quinn told the woman. But it was too late and they both knew it.

She blew a kiss and followed Frank into the back of the car. The blue Buick moved out into traffic, heading east toward Yonge Street.

Quinn watched it for a second, then began to walk quickly in the other direction.

When he heard the explosion, he was surprised. He wondered why Frank had waited three minutes before opening the briefcase.

*   *   *   *   *

At the post office, Quinn shuffled in line, then gave the card to a clerk.

The package, about the size of two telephone books, was wrapped carefully in heavy brown paper and tied with string.

Quinn flashed some ID, then signed the receipt book. The clerk stamped the card, the book and anything else he could find.

Outside the post office, Quinn took a deep breath. He was in the middle of another when the red-nosed cop plucked the package from his arms.

"Ah, Quinn," he said, "I knew ya wouldn't disappoint me."

Quinn wished he could think of something to say.

The cop moved toward the street. As he stepped off the curb, Quinn yelled: "God'll get you."

The cop laughed. The Spadina bus nailed him front and centre.

Quinn didn't feel anything. Not at first, anyway. Then he felt sick. One of the wheels had squished the cop's head like the proverbial overripe melon. But Quinn's eyes were fixed on the torn package and the bundles of cutout newspaper blowin' in the wind.

*   *   *   *   *

The answer, when it came, made Quinn throw his newspaper across the room.

He was on the couch, chuckling over the story of a Cleveland father who, on taking his young daughter to the bathroom, discovered a python, its tongue sticking out, in the toilet bowl. (The headline read: A POT TO HISS IN.)

It was the story at the bottom left that made Quinn cry.

POSTIE STAMPED OUT

The body of a 64-year-old Canada Post employee was found yesterday at the foot of his cellar stairs in his High Park-area home, Metro Toronto Police say.

Frederick Thomas Calabash, of Runnymede Rd., had been dead for about a week when his body was discovered by two boys trying to retrieve a baseball that had gone through a basement window, police said.

Calabash, a supervisor at Postal Station X on Spadina Ave., was to have retired next month.

"It's the old 'did he fall or was he pushed?' story," one homicide detective said.

Neighbors said they thought Calabash's wife, Hester, was visiting her sister in Calgary.

Police said Calabash's co-workers were not alarmed by his absence because they believed he had already retired.

Ted Wood

A former cop, Ted Wood is also former Chariman
of the Crime Writers of Canada. His first novel,
Dead In The Water, won the Scribner's Crime
Novel Award in 1983, and he's been nominated
three times for the Crime Writers of Canada's
Arthur Ellis Award. Twice for Best Novel (*Dead
In The Water* in 1984 and *Fool's Gold* in 1987) and
once for Best Short Story. His hero, Reid Bennett, is the one man police force in the fictional
Muskoka resort town of Murphy's Harbour.
Together with his side-kick, a German shepherd
named Sam, they patrol the streets and canals of
the area. "A Question of Proof" has the unique
distinction of being the only Reid Bennett short
story ever published.

A QUESTION OF PROOF

by Ted Wood

If Buck Travers hadn't asked me to be his best man I never would have killed him. Oh, I was mad enough to, when he took Andrea off me, even though I had never really got what you might call close to her. But we used to go around when she was home from college. And then Buck came into the liquor store where I work, in his army uniform, when she was dropping by and she dropped me.

He never said anything about it but it seemed his big dumb grin got bigger and dumber and the next thing they were getting married and would I stand up for him.

Don't get mad, get even, is my motto. I decided to kill him in the fall, when we went out for deer. It was what every man in town does, but by then Buck was out of the army, driving a gravel truck for the county and he said he wasn't going to kill things. Andrea didn't want him to. So I changed my plan.

I worked on it all through the fall and the Christmas rush and on into the winter before I hit on the perfect idea. I would come out of it looking bad, I could see that, but he would come out of it dead and that was what I wanted. Even if I never got any closer to Andrea, he never would either. He'd be paid out for what he'd done.

I suggested an ice-fishing trip, a stag weekend two weeks before he married Andrea, on Valentine's goddamn day if you can stomach that.

I set everything up carefully.

First off, I talked up a place over the border, in Canada, as the hot fishing spot. There's no need to go that far. We have plenty of ice fishing here in Michigan, but I figured to get away a piece and preferably somewhere that the police department would be a bunch of hicks.

Next thing was to invite the Huckmeyer boys along. They are about the best customers we've got at the liquor store and I wanted drinkers, heavy drinkers.

And last of all I said I'd provide the liquor. My treat. That swung it with the Huckmeyers. And Buck went along with it. Because that's what ice-fishing is for most guys, an excuse to drink. You sit in your overheated little ice hut, staring down that bathtub sized hole in the ice, and you drink.

We set off early one morning, with me driving. Good old generous Pete Williams, putting out for the car and the Canadian Club. I had a good reason for choosing Club. It was all part of my plan. And I had good reason to drive. I knew I could miss out on most of the drinking while I was behind the wheel, but I knew they'd be sucking on that bottle before we'd reached the county line.

That's what happened. I took one sip, to look sociable, but between the three of them they'd pretty near killed that first fifth by the time I pulled into Murphy's Harbour in Ontario.

I parked at the marina and left them at the car while I talked to the owner, the guy I'd phoned through the week to set this up. I'd asked him for two huts, close together. "Hot spots," I'd told him. "I want to kill some fish."

He didn't know that the fish I was talking about was the big blond guy in the mackinaw.

The marina guy drove us out, a mile over the lake, to the little village of fishing huts, in his four-wheel drive.

He dropped us at the edge of the row of huts and the Huckmeyers took that one and me and Buck went the fifteen paces to the next one. It was wickedly cold, 30 below anyway, and a northwest wind that would have taken your teeth out. That ice must have been two foot thick.

Perhaps you've never seen an ice hut, the way they make them in Ontario. They're built from two sheets of ply on their sides, with another two for the roof. The ends are closed in with plywood and there's a door and a small window in one end.

Me and Buck got down almost on our knees and went in. It was already warm. The marina owner had lit the stove earlier. The stove is always home-made, from sheet metal, about the size of the tins that cookies used to come in to the grocery.

The furnishings are pretty spare. There's the stove, a pile of chips for fuel, a wide bench, two tip-up fishing rigs and some bait. And there's a five-foot by two-foot hole in the ice. That's it.

Buck said, "Hey, homey!" and took off his mackinaw. That's what happens. Outside it's fifty below maybe, but inside there's so much heat from that stove that you roast. I took my coat off as well, although I was beginning to feel cold all over from the nearness of doing what I'd come for.

"First thing we need is a shot of that rye," I said and I pulled out a fresh bottle and took a belt. It had to look good because I didn't plan to drink any more after that. That's why I chose Canadian Club. It comes in a dark bottle so it's harder to see the level.

Buck matched me and we set up our rigs and sat on the bench, and started to drink in earnest.

I made a big thing about catching up, forcing the pace with the shots but turning my head away so he couldn't see that I wasn't swallowing any of it.

He wasn't suspicious. Why should he be? Here was the good sport loser, drinking with the good sport winner of the only good-looking girl in Masefield County. He thought it was real friendly. That big turkey.

He was normally no kind of a drinker. Oh he'd have a couple of beers when he took Andrea to the dance on Saturday, but never much liquor. I wasn't a drinker either. It's a bad habit to get into working in the store. But you learn to look like you approve of it so you can encourage people to buy, or in this case, to drink themselves dead.

After the first few shots he started to taper off but I kept the pressure on. "Hey," he said, his voice already a bit slurred. "I never figured you for a drinker, Pete. You bin practicin' at work?"

"I got hidden depths," I said, banging him on the arm. "An' they're all empty. I'm drownin' my sorrows."

For a moment I thought I'd blown it. He went kind of quiet and said, "Yeah, that's the on'y thing makes me sad 'bout marryin' Andrea. She used to be your girl."

"Ne'er mind," I said, like a real drunk. "Yer a goo' guy an' you'll look after 'er." And I raised the bottle and said, "To Buck an' Andrea, my bes' frien's." And I faked another pull.

He looked at me and you know what, there was a damnfool tear in his eye. And he shook my hand and said, "Gimme that," and took the bottle and said, "To Andrea and Petie, my bes' frien's." And he took a real long gurgle.

Petie! For crissakes.

Anyway, that's how it went until the fifth was gone, and he's had just about all of it, without knowing. So I brought out another one from my pack but he flapped his hand at me, all limp, like a drunk fruit and said, "Hell no, I ain' havin' no more. I'll heva li'l nap."

So I said, "Hell, i's hot. I'm gonna take my shirt off." So I did, and then my pants so I was down to my long johns like some TV hillbilly. Buck laughed like a loon and did the same. And I knew I had him.

My plan was to dare him to duck himself down the hole to get cool. It would have been easy then to keep him under. But I didn't need to. He was so drunk he passed right out.

I just rolled him head first off the bench and down the hole in the ice.

He never even woke up. I swear his eyes were shut when he went into the water. I remember thinking that the next thing he saw would be the Pearly Gates.

That was when I was the most scared. I wanted him way clear of that hole in the ice. I was afraid one of the Huckmeyers might catch a fish and come over to show us and find me on my side, reaching down under the water, making sure he was not going to bob back up and make a liar of me. I had even bought three sections of steel rod with me. I screwed them together and felt all around the hole until I was sure he was gone.

Believe me, that water was colder than anything you can imagine. But I lay there probing until I was certain it was OK. I figure he must have sunk. He gasped as he went in and that must have emptied his lungs.

When I was sure it was safe, I let go of the steel rod and sat back up to do the other things I'd planned.

First of all I swished my mouth around with the rye then spat it out and tipped most of the bottle down the hole and mixed it up until you couldn't tell it was in there.

I set the heel of the bottle down with the other empty. They were my alibi. A couple of good old boys had been boozing it up pretty good and one of them got foolish.

Then I put my boots on and, still in my long johns, I went out into the cold and ran over to the Huckmeyer's hut.

Billie opened it when I banged on the door. He was down to his undershirt. Cal was stretched out on the bunk in his long johns, snoring, the way Buck had been before I rolled him in. They had been hitting the rye pretty good themselves, but not as bad as Buck or, as far as they knew, as me.

"She here yet?" I shouted and laughed like a fool. Billie laughed as well and then asked, "Who?"

"Buck. He jus' jumped through the ice, said he'd swim over here an' scare the bejesus outa you two drunks."

That woke Cal and the whole panic started.

First thing we did was to run to all the other ice huts and see if Buck had come up through their ice hole by mistake. We all, especially me, got more excited and worried by the minute.

The result was that half an hour later we were in the drab little cinder block police station at Murphy's Harbour talking to their police department.

It's a one-man, one-dog outfit. The chief's named Bennett. A tall, rangy kind of guy in his late thirties. He looked like a hick and I figured I was safe, but I kept to my plan.

He just sat there with that big German shepherd beside him while I went over and over the story.

The way I told it was that me and my good old buddy, Buck, had been drinking, in celebration of his coming marriage.

He made me stop and go over the drinking in detail. How much of what we had drunk in how long. By then he had already been out to the ice hut and had even reached down under the ice himself so he really knew about the two fifths of Club. But he asked me every time and when I spelled it out for him, forgetful and stumbling, like any drunk I'd seen in the store, he would squinch his eyes up and whistle.

"Go on," he said, every time, and I did. I explained that we got very warm and took our heavy clothes off and then Buck had this great idea. He was always a good swimmer, from the old swimming hole days, so that part stood up. He was going to swim across to the Huckmeyers and scare the hell outa them.

"And what did you say?" The chief kept his voice flat as the eyes of his big dog. If I hadn't planned everything so carefully, I would have been scared then. I said, "Well, you know, I said, 'Hell, that's crazy, Buck'."

"But he did it anyway."

"Yeah. He was a tough guy, Buck. He was in th' army." The chief grinned, like a crack forming on the lake ice. "So was I." he said. "But it doesn't qualify you to duck under the ice and swim around."

"We was drunk," I said sadly. "I was, too. Otherwise I woulda stopped him some way."

"Sure," Bennett said, and he sounded satisfied.

He told me to wait a while and went out to talk to the Huckmeyers in the front of the office.

I sat there sweating, looking into the cold eyes of that big black and tan dog of his and listening to the murmur of voices until he came back.

He sat down again and asked me about Buck.

"You were a good buddy of his?"

"He was my bes' frien'. I was gonna be his bes' man." And for good measure I threw in a touch of the bereaved drunk. "Now warram I gonna tell 'is girl?"

"Her name is Andrea Walters?" the chief asked, in the same quiet voice.

"Howja know?"

"Your friends told me." He let this rest a minute until I was beginning to get scared, then he said, "They tell me you and she used to be pretty close."

"Kind of. We wen' out a while."

I was prepared for that one. It was no use protesting I had never known Andrea. I was just anxious not to sound as if I'd been cut out. That would have been dumb, almost as dumb as encouraging a man with twenty ounces of booze in him to jump through eighteen inches of ice and find his way through the dark to another keyhole.

Then the chief did something I didn't count on. He said, "I don't envy you having to break the news to her."

It threw me and I covered up by putting my hands over my face and heaving my shoulders for a minute or two. It was an academy award performance.

He reached out gently and put his hand on my shoulder.

"That's the terrible thing about drinking," he said. "Come on, better get started."

He led me out with that silent shadow of a dog just a half step behind him. I could feel my heart lifting with every step towards the door. I had done it. I had killed that sonofabitch and gotten away with it. I smiled inside and thanked Canadian Club for their help.

The chief led me right to the flap in the counter that let us out into the front of the office, then he stopped, with his hand on it and turned to me, looking me right in the face.

"I just thought of a problem," he said, and my pulse hammered in my throat. I covered it by a little drunken sway, nothing too grand, just a reminder of my innocence.

"Wassat?" I asked him.

"Who's gonna drive?" he asked mildly.

"'S my car," I said.

And that's when he shook his head, sad and patient. "That's what I mean," he said. "The thing is, all three of you have been drinking all day, and I mean *drinking*." He gave a little laugh that wrung a smile out of me and a little laugh out of both the Huckmeyer boys. Then he dropped it and said, "I can't let you drive, the shape you're in."

He stood there, looking at me in the same bleak way that hole in the ice had looked at me after Buck went down it. I could feel the walls closing in. I knew I had to get out of that place. I couldn't have stayed there another minute.

"I'm OK," I insisted. "The shock sobered me up damn quick."

He nodded and smiled, but not with his eyes.

"I can understand what you mean," he said. "But it would be more than my job's worth to let you drive. How about I give you a breathalizer, just for the record?"

And I said, "Sure," before I realized what I was doing.

He played me like a big fish. He tested the Huckmeyer boys first and they blew numbers that would have gotten them locked up for going near a car.

Then he tested me and found me stone cold sober. The Huckmeyers both laughed and said, "Hey, great Pete, you can drive."

The chief was writing down the results in his note book. "Not yet," he said, without looking up. Then he looked at me, through me. "I'd say you've had around two ounces all day," he said. "Which is what I figured from the clearness of your eyes. Now how about you and me have another little talk about what really happened out in that ice hut."

Elaine Mitchell Matlow

Elaine Matlow was born in Toronto. She has lived in England and Isreal where she taught English, Theatre Arts and English as a Second Language. She also taught a course on writing mystery fiction at George Brown College in Toronto. "Safe as House's" is her second published short story. The first, "To Court Disaster", appeared in the 1984 anthology *Fingerprints*, a collection of stories by members of the Crime Writers of Canada.

SAFE AS HOUSES

by Elaine Mitchell Matlow

It was a murder with style. Sam always used to talk about whether a house "showed well". You could say that his corpse showed well.

On Monday morning at dawn Sam was seen stretched out on the sloping lawn of a house he had sold on Saturday night. The sold sign -- SAM CLIFF REAL ESTATE -- 785-1111 -- FOR SALE/SOLD -- was staked through the body of Sam Cliff into the summer grass.

He hadn't been killed by the sign. He had been knifed, and then arranged on the lawn by someone with a semiotic sense of humour.

His wallet and all his belongings were untouched. Only his gold pen that he always carried with him was missing.

As Sam's wife I was the number one suspect until the police found out that almost everyone close to Sam had hated him. Then the investigators became confused. They still haven't solved Sam's murder. It is one of only three unsolved murders in the past year in Metropolitan Toronto. By coincidence, all three bodies were found outside: the infanticide in a garbage can, an unidentified rubby in a downtown alley, and Sam on a Chaplin Estates lawn.

Staff-Sergeant Pierson and Sergeant Black came to see me on Monday afternoon. It was clear to me, clear as the gentle light coming through the conservatory windows, that they had heard about the exact amount of love lost between Sam and me. They asked the questions as if they knew nothing, but they had already heard. In the first few seconds of meeting me, when Serena showed them into the conservatory, they obviously -- I could see their eyes move -- sized me up. I am five feet, eleven. Sam had been five feet five. I could have done it, physically. I had a motive. Motives. I had opportunity. I had been home alone all last night. Serena had been away for the night, staying with her boyfriend as she always did on Sunday nights.

Oh, I could have done it. But so could the Hennings, Sharon Brown, Erica Cole, Danny Drim, or my brother-in-law, Arthur. None of us had alibis for Sam's probable time of death.

And any of us might have wanted to do it. I confess to a lifting of the heart when I took a detour past the Henning house later in the day and saw the sold sign on the lawn. It was a duplicate sold sign by then, of course, and Sam's body was not splayed beneath it. But I could imagine the scene at dawn like a still from a movie.

Staff-Sergeant Pierson, thin, long, and fine-boned, leaned back in my Le Corbusier black leather chair as if he belonged there, and asked me about my separation from Sam. I answered truthfully although I was aware of their suspicion of me.

"We haven't lived together for over a year." They would know that anyway. "Sam was living with his girlfriend, Erica Cole, and he was planning to marry her, as far as I know, when our divorce came through."

"What led to your separation?" asked Sergeant Black. He was stockier than Pierson, with a broad face and slit-like black eyes.

"I outgrew him. You see, he was totally amoral." I wanted these men to understand but I couldn't see much affect in their eyes. "When I first fell in love with Sam I couldn't see what he was really like because he could be so charming. He was very good at gauging how well he was taking another person in." I smiled. Pierson smiled back. "An asset in real estate but not in marriage."

"When did you first realize that he was short on morals?" asked Pierson.

"It didn't happen all at once. He gradually realized that he wasn't fooling me any longer, that there was nothing to be gained from a bit more charm, and the marriage was over. We stayed together for the sake of the house. I never did leave him. He left me. For Erica. After years of fooling around, he fell in love." I tried to say that lightly.

"Did you hate him for that?"

"Oh, no, I was relieved. I wanted to leave but I kept putting it off. It scared me to make such a decisive move. It wasn't only this," I waved to indicate the house, and by extension, the money. "But it is true that I had every comfort, open access to his account, my own bedroom suite. He demanded very little from me. He wanted very little from me."

"Then why did you consider leaving"

I smiled again. "I didn't like myself for being supported by a snake, for being connected to him."

The two cops exchanged a glance. I knew what it meant. It's a mistake to be open about complex emotional issues with people who are worrying about their next mortgage payment and think you're spoiled. But I felt I had to be honest with the police.

"What about the house?" asked Sergeant Black. "Would you have been able to keep it if you were divorced?

"No, but I wouldn't have cared." My first lie. "With half the proceeds of this house I think I could have found another I liked almost as well." I hoped they picked up the irony. "I certainly wouldn't have murdered him for this house."

That was true, barely. I wouldn't have murdered Sam just to be able to keep our wonderful house on Russell Hill Road, but I did love it. I had grown up in a flat near Kensington Market with three sisters and a mother and father who were always sad, tired, and angry, sometimes too sad and tired to be angry. The three-story Georgian style house with its natural charm, well-proportioned rooms, light and space (not to mention the extensive renovations and Italian tiled pool) gave me a daily joy that would have been hard to give up.

I especially love the conservatory. The three outer walls and the ceiling are of beautiful old garden glass with lines and bubbles. The floor is a perfect blue-green grey slate, the colour of "subtle", as one of my friends remarked. A few old Persian carpets, leather furniture (two chairs are copies of Jacques Ruhlmann's 1926 Elephant chair) and built-in bookshelves all around the lower third of the room give warmth to the huge room.

I have never had a peak experience in sex or in nature. But I sometimes get that feeling of being at one with the world, of being transfused by quiet joy in that room. A view of the pool, a glance at my well-loved books, a breathing in of the colour of the slate, the quiet exuberance of the light, a cup of freshly ground Blue Mountain coffee, and I am entirely happy.

Or I had been until the police came. It's not by accident that you never see policemen on the pages of Architectural Digest or House and Garden. The fantasy of comfort and elegance is somewhat jarred by these symbols of order. Order in the greater society, perhaps. But disorder, at least for awhile, in the lives of those inhabitants of the rooms where they sit and question.

When they left I made myself another cup of coffee, but my mood was disturbed. I felt agitated. My calm world had been shaken and I could not measure out the rest of my day in the usual pleasant pursuits. Thank goodness I had been able to keep my nail appointment with Yolanda this morning. My nails had been a mess and I wanted to look good at the funeral the next day. I phoned the hospital and told Mrs. Murphy that I couldn't come in to read stories to the kids in the opthalmic wing as I usually do on Monday afternoons, and then phoned Sharon Brown and asked her to come for tea. She told me that the police were at her place but that after they left she would be able to come over.

Sharon and I have been friendly for a long time. I knew that Sam had been sleeping with Sharon for years, and didn't mind at all after a while. Sam's infatuation for Erica was far more of a shock for Sharon than for me, and somehow, oddly, but not oddly, I was the person Sharon felt could best understand her feelings of hurt and betrayal when Sam dumped her. Sam had of course been talking marriage to Sharon. He always told people what they wanted to hear.

I had Serena lay out some cheeses and crackers on a tray while I drove out to Paul's shop in the village (taking my detour past the Hennings on route) to get some fruit tarts. I ran into Shelley Gladstone there. She was glowing with only slightly suppressed excitement.

"Hi, Susan. I'm dreadfully sorry about Sam." She looked like a sunbeam dancing on a wave. "What a terrible tragedy." Her eyes shone.

"Yes, it was." I couldn't blame Shelley. She hated Sam too.

She had dealt with him when she bought her house on Elderwood. Sam had sent his tame house inspector over to give her the word on the condition of the house before she put in an offer. Sam's inspector found the house to be in excellent condition. (He found all of Sam's houses to be in excellent condition.) For the next year, although she did make a pretense of stopping when I came into the locker room, she regaled our tennis club with the continuing saga of the roof that had to be replaced (after the baby raccoons were removed) of the chimneys that had to be rebuilt, the weeping tiles that had to be put in all around the house, and assorted plumbing and electrical problems.

Shelley danced around me for a few minutes, like a boxer now, hoping to put in a thumb and pull out a plum, but I was discretion itself. I could be more open with Sharon.

We clinked Waterford glasses of pink champagne. "To his executioner!" toasted Sharon and we laughed. You don't have to be a murderer to enjoy the fact that Sam was killed. I had grown to hate him slowly through the years, and Sharon had come to hate him in one day, the day he announced to all his staff that he had fallen in love with Erica and would be living with her. Everyone there knew he had been sleeping with Sharon, and that she had been hoping for marriage. Everyone, some sympathetic, a few merely unpleasantly curious, watched Sharon not fall apart in front of them.

And then Sharon had to continue working for Sam. She was divorced, two children, and not well off. The real estate market was slow then. It would have been hard for her to change firms.

"Did they ask where you were last night?"

"Yes," I answered. "I don't have an alibi."

"Me, neither." She sighed. "Is it possible that he's going to be as much trouble dead as he was alive?" We giggled. Sharon is very good company, and we had become closer since the day he disappointed and humiliated her in the lobby (done in the latest pink and turquoise, with California shutters) of the Sam Cliff Real Estate Company offices.

The next day I saw Sharon again, as well as the other nine agents of Sam's company, my sister Carole, my brother-in-law Arthur, my nephews, Erica Cole, Danny Drim, and the Hennings at Sam's funeral.

Erica was dressed to overkill in a little black Valentino number that she must have rushed out and bought yesterday. Her makeup was carefully blended from the purple-grey palette, and with her long dark hair and her dramatic white skin she was stunning. Young and stunning.

Sharon was dressed well enough in an old black suit. She always bought one good item at the sales and with care and energy she managed to be well turned out. All the agents at Sam's firm dressed well, some with more flair, some with less, but all aware that their credibility as house agents depended to some extent on appearance.

Danny Drim, who headed a rival real estate agency, and who was Sam's well-known enemy and phony buddy, was also nattily turned out. He wasn't even bothering to look sad. His wife had often enough been impaled by Sam -- Danny might well have wanted to return that favour. He smiled and joked with everyone before the service began. Propriety had never much influenced Danny. Our two policemen seemed to be watching him particularly closely.

The Hennings had appropriate expressions on their faces, but they had hated Sam too. They were a young couple, both lawyers, who had just sold the small house with the large lawn which had sported Sam's body. Sam had shafted them royally over the house deal, and it made sense that one or both of them could have returned the favour. Certainly Sharon had overheard James Henning tell Sam that he'd like to kill him. But that only meant something in the light of what happened. Otherwise, telling Sam that you wanted to kill him was everyday talk in his life. People said it to him all the time. He liked it. It meant he had got the better of a deal.

My sister and brother-in-law and their three boys were sitting directly behind me. They were here out of "respect". But I knew how much Arthur had wanted to move to a larger house -- two cats, a dog, a bird, a gerbil, two white rats and three children were making their three bedroom house seem tight -- Sam had laughed at him. "You can't afford it. If you want to be a professor, then live like a professor!"

Arthur and Carole and the kids eventually did move to a larger house, and Sam charged Arthur the usual 6% M.L.S. commission, although he had earlier promised to charge only 3%. There was nothing Arthur could do. There was nothing I could do. When Jeffrey, my oldest nephew, began to worship his dashing, successful Uncle Sam and to question Arthur's values in a nasty adolescent way, Arthur *really* began to hate Sam. Yet I know that Arthur couldn't have murdered anyone. He's on the board of the Abolition of the Death Penalty Society and of Canadians Against Nuclear War. He even rescues bees and bugs from the swimming pool when they come over to visit.

Sam's divorce lawyer, Ian Carstairs, was there too, looking very smooth. He was known as a killer in matrimonial battles, and he certainly had been out to get Sam the best deal he could. Fairness or my rights were of no interest to him. I had made the mistake of hiring a female lawyer who was more conciliatory and less aggressive. I liked her but I had been thinking of firing her before Sam was killed.

During the eulogy I had trouble keeping a straight face. I was sitting in the front row and I turned again to look at the gathering to steady me. To my surprise Erica was silently crying. She really must have loved Sam. She would have been disillusioned later, but at least by dying now Sam had one true mourner.

Maybe two. Jeffrey looked as if he were choking back tears. Arthur looked as if he would like to choke *him*. The two detectives were in the back row, taking the whole thing in.

"It was a nice funeral," Black commented when they came to see me the next day. "We noticed that your nephew was very upset."

"He loved his Uncle Sam."

"We know," said Pierson, leaning back comfortably in my favourite Brunschwig & Fils reupholstered chair in the living room. "We talked to him last evening and he told us how good his uncle had been to him and how angry that had made his father. Your brother-in-law was angry at Sam for many reasons, wasn't he?"

"Not very angry," I replied stiffly. "Not murderously angry."

"We've heard differently."

"People will always talk and Arthur was open about his dislike of Sam. But he's really a lovely guy."

"What about the Hennings," continued Pierson. Black was checking out the art in the living room. He was staring at my new Judi Lenerman, perhaps trying to reconcile its daring colours and lines with the more orthodox Miro and Chagall prints that Sam and I had bought together to decorate the room.

"I hardly know them. I think their lawn was chosen just because someone wanted to use a sold sign."

"There are a lot of Sam Cliff sold signs around, though. And the Hennings could have wanted revenge on Sam."

"What do you mean?"

"We heard what Sam did to the Hennings. Didn't you know?"

"I heard some of it. A lot of Sam Cliff gossip got back to me."

"Then you know how they paid much more than they should have for their new house."

"Yes. An offer came in at the same time as theirs, and they panicked. They didn't negotiate."

"Right. A false offer."

"A Sam Cliff special offer. He did it all the time."

"And they would have made thirty thousand more on their

own house if they had accepted the first offer they got, and it's what they wanted to do. But Sam strongly advised them not to accept the first offer. He convinced them."

Had Sharon been talking? "Sam could be very convincing."

"So I gather," replied Pierson. "Sam didn't want them to take that offer because it was brought in by a LePage agent and he didn't want to split the commission with another agency. He wanted one of his own agents to bring in an offer. So he persuaded the Hennings that better offers would come in later and that they should wait."

"Then the market crashed."

"That's right." He nodded at me. "What beats me is why Sam would care so much about a deal that was pretty small potatoes. He was a wealthy man."

"You had to know Sam. That's how he got to be so wealthy. Every deal was crucial to him. He'd work the small ones as hard as the big ones. He played tennis that way too. He played people that way."

"And he was wealthy?" Pierson asked gently.

"Very."

"He wasn't caught in the up-and-down market of the last few years?"

"I know nothing about that."

"Really? Ian Carstairs, his lawyer, told us that Sam's income was only thirty-one thousand last year. Did you know that?"

"Yes." I crossed my legs and reached for a Sobranie Black & Gold. "As you probably know, my lawyer apprised me of Sam's income".

"Carstairs wouldn't say so but it was obvious that Sam's declared income might have been different from his real income. What would you say his real income was -- two hundred thousand?"

"I have no idea. I never did know."

"Perhaps not. But what you would know is that on thirty-one thousand a year of declared income you would get very little maintenance. Half the proceeds of this house, if you're lucky, and after real estate agent's fees," Pierson smiled pleasantly, "would be about four hundred and twenty-five thousand. Not even enough to buy a condo in this area or to have any money to invest for income. Quite a change in your lifestyle."

I stared straight at him. "I was very poor when I was growing up. I could make do on four hundred thousand."

"Oh, you could. Most of the world could. But did you want to?"

* * * * *

I learned through the gossip network, some information on the phone with Sharon, a little more during a hair treatment at Mary Trippi, still some more during a lunch at Dunkleman's, bits and pieces at the tennis club, more at 21 McGill, even more in a chance encounter at Paul's French Food Shoppe, that the police had questioned everyone with a motive, even those with not much of a motive. But I learned that eventually they had to drop the case, and eventually everyone stopped talking about it. It became just one of those unsolved cases of the past year.

Until last week. For some reason the police have reopened the case. Maybe it's because of pressure put on them by Erica's father. He is, after all, very rich, very well-connected politically, and a local philanthropist.

My reaction to this new turn of events is to consciously enjoy each day in my wonderful house. I have been writing a little of this in the late afternoons. I sit in a slant of quiet sunlight and make notes on the heavy handmade paper in my notebook with the 18K gold Mont Blanc fountain pen, broad nib, black ink.

I have always been good at enjoying the small pleasures of the moment, and I feel perfectly unworried and content as I sit in my favourite mouse gray leather chair in the conservatory, a cup of chocolate Brazilian coffee from Dinah's cupboard on the side table, Mozart's Clarinet Quintet as background music, and my burgundy tooled leather notebook on my lap.

Jas. R. Petrin

James Petrin was born in Antler, Saskatchewan in 1947 and now lives in Winnipeg. Since 1985, when his first story "The Smile", appeared in *Alfred Hitchcock Mystery Magazine* he's been a regular contributor. Two of his stories, "Magic Nights" and "Prairie Heat" were short-listed for the Crime Writers of Canada'a Arthur Ellis Award/Amphora Prize in 1988. And in 1989 Petrin's "Killer in the House" won the Short Story Arthur. His "Dark Shoes" is a classic story of detection and startling revelation.

DARK SHOES

by Jas. R. Petrin

"Those," said Overdale with authority, pointing through the window glass, "are sling-backs. Those low ones are espadrilles, those are stiletoes. And those are mules."

Wilde stood back in amazement and studied his good friend with new respect. "Women's shoes? I'm impressed. How the devil did you come to know so much about that subject?"

"An old case," Overdale told him. "I've impressed myself, actually, with my own powers of recall. That sad death took place some years ago."

"Death?" Wilde was now all ears. They turned together and walked on down the street through a muggy June day. People were plentiful, hurrying past the shops with rapid steps; Wilde found himself suddenly noticing the passing female footwear. "Tell me more. You haven't mentioned a word about this case before."

Each day the two men made this walk. Now they stopped and bought their customary ice cream from the Eezy-Freeze vendor and found a shady bench in the plaza, opposite the entrance to an air-conditioned mall where they could observe the knots of shoppers come and go. No duties beckoned them, for both were retirees -- Overdale previously a Detective Inspector, born and trained in England, but late of the Winnipeg police; Wilde a private investigator who had lived and worked all his life in the West. Having retired here to Marsten in the Pembina Hills some years before, they had met in the apartment building which they shared, had exchanged introductions and been friends ever since.

"Before you start, though," Wilde said, "give me the principal players. I like to see 'em as flesh and blood."

Overdale nodded, and his gaze wandered among the hurrying shoppers as though seeking there those unhappy figures of so many years ago. He was a close man -- stand-offish, some would say -- and if pressed he would admit that he preferred the human individual to humankind. Still, his many years spent in dealings with the worst side of society had not made him a cynic.

"I suppose I should begin with Hartney. He was the dead woman's lover, and the most obvious suspect once the likelihood of suicide began to fade. A man reluctantly dragging his heels into middle age, affecting youth in his clothing, in the cut of his hair. And, in fact, he did appear a good ten years younger than his wife, if you didn't trouble too much about his eyes, which had a harried weariness that gave him away on the spot. He had no criminal record to speak of, though he'd been in trouble as a boy for maltreatment of animals --"

"Maltreatment of animals?"

"Yes. It seems that he and a few school chums would take cats up to a third floor balcony and drop them over the side to see how they managed the sudden stop. Or by way of variation, kick them into storm sewers to test their swimming abilities. Young experimenters -- juvenile Pavlovs. They were caught and repri-manded, and nothing more came of it.

"He met his wife at high school. She wasn't his sort at all -- not a pretty girl, I mean: she looked positively bleak in the school photo I saw, a squat little tank of a thing. But her father owned the bakeshop then, and who knows? Maybe to the young Hartney a bakeshop was independence and security beyond imagining. In any case, they did marry and eventually inherited her father's business, though their wedded life was far from blissful. She was ill-tempered and jealous -- not without cause, it turned out -- and she left the bakeshop after a time, preferring to work in a clothing factory. Soon after that, Hartney took up with Rona Cleary. He did seem to feel deeply for the girl, by the way -- and right from the first he argued strenuously against the suggestion of suicide."

"And what was *she* like?"

Overdale tilted his head and squinted; he might have just spotted her coming up the street.

"A pretty thing. Petite, bright, with a flare for style. Too short for a model, she'd planned to become a fashion consultant. A tragic thing, her death; but then it always is on the victim's side of the balance. She was born in Windsor or Detroit -- I forget which -- and when her father deserted the family her mother came out west and eventually met and married Cleary. Her new home life was not all it could have been -- John Cleary was a tyrant, by all accounts. But she rose above it somehow, was goodnatured and pleasant to everyone. I learned all this by asking questions; when I made my own acquaintance with the poor girl she was already hanging by her neck in a rough shed at the back of Hartney's shop."

There was a note of sadness in Overdale's voice. Although neither man had married, Wilde knew that his friend would have liked children of his own, and was equally sure he'd have been a good father to them. Overdale's amiable features hardened as he began a description of John Cleary.

"Did you ever meet a man who seemed at first sight the epitomy of brutishness? That was Cleary to me. A man who might have been raised in a cage and fed with raw meat. I admit I was prejudiced: one always wants to blame the parents for harm that befalls the child; 'Where were *you* when it happened?' one wants to say. He was uncommunicative -- almost dour, and made you feel as you do in the proximity of a dog that's been known to bite. A janitor most of his life, he worked at a soap factory after losing a good position in the schools over some trivial thing -- perhaps he bit the principal. He had a good fifteen years on his wife, and was almost forty years older than the deceased." Overdale made his next point by glaring at Wilde in defiance, "Child-rearing should be left to the young -- it's the natural arrangement."

That social comment off his chest, he resettled himself.

"What else can I say about Cleary? He liked to garden -- a solitary pursuit. As for friends, I heard about one: a florid man who ranted himself into a massive coronary; Cleary didn't even go to the funeral; of what use to him was a dead friend? His idea of a weekend was to lay in a store of beer and drink it alone in a dark room, crushing the caps between thumb and fore-finger as they came off the bottles and hurling them at the wall. On his best days he tended his garden, and at night he went for walks."

"Humm," Wilde said, "I can see why the girl wanted better company."

"Hartney was no prince."

"He might've been to her."

"Perhaps. Anyway, you're right that Rona Cleary had little to look for at home. Her own mother saw her as an encumbrance. A dull, vindictive person, perhaps was just the woman for a boor like Cleary: she could hurl words like poisoned darts. It was her, by the way, that alerted me to Hartney's misspent youth. And she added something else; that there had been an assault on the local cat population just weeks before Rona died."

Wilde raised an eyebrow.

"Wait a minute. You did say Hartney was approaching middle age. You aren't suggesting he'd suddenly started in on cats again after all that time?"

"Mrs. Cleary thought he had. She knew about his juvenile indiscretions through her husband, who had been custodian at Hartney's school when it happened."

"Humm! And these other cats -- the more recent batch. Were they found in a neat pile under Hartney's top-floor window?"

"No. Throttled this time. Hung from the fenceposts in the lane with the same strong twine that ended the life of Rona Cleary." He paused. "And the same twine, incidentally, that was dispensed in Hartney's bakeshop."

"Fantastic."

"I agree. Still, Mrs. Cleary suspected -- no, that isn't strong enough -- was *convinced* that this proved Hartney was a murderer, a man who had killed her daughter with a cruelty stemming from barbarous attacks upon cats. That he'd furthered an old penchant for sadistic cruelty by murdering her poor Rona."

"A broad leap for a penchant, and for logic."

"Not for her. And you have to admit to the linkage, the progression. As a boy, a man mistreats cats. He becomes an adult and cats are despatched near his home, throttled with twine from his own shop. Then his lover is found hanged with that twine from a beam in his shed. Pretty damning. Once Mrs. Cleary filled me in on all of this -- whatever her motivation -- I had to alter my conviction that the girl was a suicide."

"Well, with due respect," Wilde said, "the second incident with the cats provides the only linkage with what Hartney did as a kid. Take that away and your progression falls apart. Can you say more about that part of the business?"

"Yes. It began in the early spring," Overdale said. "The first feline casualty belonged to a neighbour of the Hartneys -- a Mrs. Bates? ...Gates? It doesn't matter. She got worried when her fat orange Tom didn't come yowling at the door one morning, as was its custom. She went looking, found it hanging from her own back gate, the twine knotted around its neck. As you'd expect, she screamed like the devil and brought the neighbourhood running. A day or two later another cat met the same fate. And after that, another -- then another. Conclusions were drawn from the twine at that point, and goaded on by Mrs. Cleary the local cat-owners were in an uproar, after Hartney's hide. Then, as suddenly as it had begun, the serial cat-killing stopped. People assumed that whoever was responsible had grown tired of the game. And I suppose in a sense they were right."

"How many cats got despatched -- total?" Wilde asked.

"Five, I think."

"And where was Hartney during it all? Did he have an alibi -- out of town, sick in bed, that sort of thing?"

"No, he didn't. I checked later, after Mrs. Cleary's accusation, and he couldn't come up with any worthwhile excuses at all. But then he wasn't the sickly type, and he rarely went anywhere."

"Getting away from the cats, what was your gut feeling? Could he have killed the girl?"

"Yes, but I didn't think so -- you see, he'd hurt his hand; but I'll come to that later."

Wilde plucked at his chin, puzzling aloud. He shook his head. "Hanging's a damned awkward way to kill somebody. But if Hartney killed the girl and staged her suicide, he'd have wanted to reinforce the idea of self-destruction, not argue against it as you say he did. He could have claimed later that they'd had a falling out, that he'd warned her he was breaking it off; no one could dispute what he may have said to a dead woman. And it would have given her a believable reason for suicide -- a woman spurned, and all that." He broke off. "But if you've got all your ducks in a row, let's have the story -- from the top."

"I was a young fellow then," Overdale said, "not long off the boat from Jolly Old, newly assigned to Homicide, and I'd never seen a dead woman before. A few men killed in fights or accidents, but never a dead woman, and certainly not a hanged one."

As Overdale settled into his story, Wilde found himself quickly carried away by it. They had contrived a sort of game over the years, one man relating a crime he had worked on while the other listened to the clues, trying to solve it. Wilde liked listening to Overdale, who had a strong mellow voice and a good delivery. "It was in the north end of the city, one of those streets lined with tall peaked houses and having a bakery or a sausage shop at almost every corner. The weather was gusty, as I recall -- the poplars bending low at the waist and showing their silver backs to the wind. The neighbours were gathering like ravens, and I needed two constables to keep them away. Entering the shed, I could see that the hanging was clumsily done, with the tiny knuckle of the knot positioned at the back of the head, tilting the chin sharply forward over the breast. She was -- had been -- a pretty woman; you could still see that in spite of the dark protruding tongue. It was Hartney who'd discovered the body."

Wilde broke in, "Naturally, you suspected him at once."

"No. Not then. I should have, I see that now. But at first glance it was such an obvious case of suicide. Let me try to describe it. Imagine a very large old shed, sloped ceiling, stout open beams crossing overhead at intervals, from one of which the poor woman hung like a sack. She wore a crisp white dress with a red belt, her hair all in waves as was the fashion then. Eyeshadow, lipstick, fingernail polish. A strong packaging twine had been doubled back upon itself a number of times to form the rope which was stretched taut over its beam, one end in the knot at her neck, the other fixed to the steel leg of a work bench. A stool was overturned beneath her and a pair of black high-heeled shoes were nearby on the floor. There was something that struck me as strange about the shoes, some elusive oddness that I couldn't quite grasp."

"Aha," said Wilde, "sort of scattered, like she'd kicked 'em off while struggling..."

"No. Not like that at all. They were neatly positioned side by side, as if in a clothes closet. Even the little buckles of the straps were done up. It wasn't so curious an arrangement for a suicide. I presumed she had taken them off before climbing up onto the stool -- as you know, people will do odd, tidy things like that when contriving to end their existence. I made all the notes I could, then let the photographers in with their gear, the medical examiner's people and the rest of them. The body was cut down, there were measurements taken, all that sort of thing."

"What kind?"

"Pardon?"

"Since you raised the subject, what kind of shoes were they?"

"Oh, stilettoes. Sling-backed and open-toed. Black leather. Expensive. I learned all that later. At the time they were simply shoes."

"And no handbag?"

Overdale smiled appreciatively. "You're awake, aren't you? No, there was no handbag. But don't infer too much from that. She only lived a few doors down."

"You questioned this guy Hartney right then?"

"Of course."

"And did he seem adequately grief-stricken?"

Overdale settled back on the bench, draped one leg over another and gave his attention back to the hurrying shoppers and his melting ice cream.

"I asked him for an eyewitness account of the scene just as he'd found it. He described it pretty much as I had noted it myself, with the exception that he didn't seem to know just what position the shoes were in. This didn't surprise me: the average person is not a trained observer. I spoke to Mrs. Hartney as well, but all I got from her was a gush of support for her husband: she was adamant it was a suicide, kept repeating the word. She perceived the difficulty her husband was in before any of us.

"Was Hartney suitably distraught? I judged that he was, but as I say I was young at the time. I was pretty certain the death was a suicide, and was ready to report it as such if the autopsy turned up no oddities and confirmed the apparent cause of death. And it did confirm it -- congestion and tiny hemorrhages in the eyeballs and the face; death caused by obstruction of the blood supply, and no other marks on the body other than the deep welts of the twine.

"It *looked* like a suicide. Had all the earmarks. And as you said yourself, hanging is a troublesome method of murder. To bring it off one has to be vastly more powerful than one's victim. Also, there was no indication of violent struggle in the room or on the body. But for the absence of a letter or a note, it was the classic scene. What made me reconsider was new information that soon came to light. Not evidence -- you'd scarcely call it that: more an allegation."

"Allegation," Wilde echoed, liking the sound of the word.

"An allegation over the telephone," Overdale added. "Mrs. Cleary with her story about the cats. After hearing her out I could tell she was something of a Dragon Lady, and I knew that her tirade might be merely a slander. But it did make me realize that I may have been too quick to accept the cause of death as suicide."

Overdale then went to have more words with the dead woman's lover, Hartney. This time it was a more formal interview, conducted in the Hartney's apartment, a cramped menage of three or four stuffy rooms over his shop. He was a baker, the Hartneys had no air conditioning, and the apartment was as hot as an oven: Hartney could have baked his bread in the kitchen sink. But though the heat was oppresive Overdale wanted to question husband and wife seperately, and this day was opportune as Mrs. Hartney was at her job in a downtown dress factory.

"They were a gloomy set of rooms," Overdale said, "infused with the air of resigned unhappiness. It was clear to me that the marriage was a bad one, clear from her neglect of the housekeeping -- days-old food scraps in the sink; and in his neglect of the chores -- a broken sofa leg, a missing windowpane carelessly fitted with cardboard. There were shelves lined with paperback mysteries. Hartney himself could have been the dead woman's father, a man of thirty-odd years who cultivated a student's appearance, with narrow jeans and T-shirt sleeves rolled up tight, one of them showing the square bulge of a tucked away cigarette pack as they carried them at that time. He looked fatigued, with smoker's wrinkles about his eyes, and had a nervous habit of pulling at his watchband. Also, he had apparently sustained a recent injury: his right hand was swathed in white gauze from the second joint of the fingers to the wrist. He seated me in the living room, excavating a spot among the abandoned newspapers and food wrappers with his good hand; he half-heartedly offered me tea, then excused himself saying he couldn't locate a clean cup.

"First of all, Mr. Hartney," I began, "I'd like to know when you first came to know Miss Cleary, and some of the circumstances of that meeting."

He shrugged. "Rona was a customer. A beautiful girl I thought when I first saw her, and a stylish dresser. She came into the shop wanting bagels. I don't make bagels, and told her so -- told her she'd have to go to New York if she wanted good ones. She laughed and said that I ought to make them, that she had a recipe for them which might interest me. I told her to bring it along next time she came, and she went straight home and got it. She was lively, always quick to laugh. Bubbly, you know? I liked that. We got to discussing baking -- and everything started from there, I guess."

"You said it surprised you that she would take her own life."

He became suddenly animated.

"Yes. Yes, it damn well does. It's not her way at all. I'm no psychologist, but I think I would have seen some sign in her of that sort of violence coming. She never hid her emotions. She was always open -- not just with me, but with everyone. Her home life was rotten, Sergeant --rotten! Her stepfather is a monster. But all the same, she could cope. She was small, but very strong on the inside, where it counts."

"Are you saying her stepfather beat her?"

"No, she never complained of that -- and I'd've seen the marks if he had." He shook his head slowly. "Suicide! Rona was the last person to do such a thing. Take my word for it."

"Your wife believes otherwise."

"She didn't know Rona at all!"

I sat for a while saying nothing, allowing the man to calm himself. Hartney had been spindling the watch band about his wrist feverishly; now he let go of it and cupped his injured hand in his good one.

"I spoke with Rona's mother over the telephone," I revealed flatly, "and I must tell you she said something which was not very flattering to you."

Hartney sighed through his nose and shook his head.

"Not that business about the cats again?"

"As a matter of fact, it was about cats. You aren't surprised?"

"No. She's been making a career of that. I'm sure she'd plaster it on the front pages of the newspapers if she could afford it. She went around at the time bad-mouthing me to the neighbours, and got them all suspecting me. All because of a stupid thing I'd done as a boy. Her vicious tongue hurt our business. I'd have sued her if hadn't been for Rona." He brushed an invisible Mrs. Cleary from the air with his hand. "Look, Sergeant, I don't know who killed those damned cats. Somebody warped, no doubt -- it was a warped thing to do. But it sure as hell wasn't me."

"They were found with twine about their necks, hanging from the fences along the back alley of this street. Exactly the same twine which you keep by the roll to tie up large bundles for your customers. You admit you had the means and the opportunity?"

His colour was rising, his cheeks getting red.

"Everybody in the damn neighbourhood had the opportunity. *And* the means. I give that twine out to dozens of customers each week."

I then said as gently as I could, "But there's a new development now. Not everybody in the neighbourhood has lost a lover by strangulation."

Hartney dropped his head into one hand and clutched at his hair. It was as if he despaired of explaining himself on the subject of cats.

I allowed him a moment, then said, "Your wife first became aware of your relationship with Miss Cleary quite recently, didn't she? Was it because you'd begun wearing the watch band that Miss Cleary gave you?"

"How did you know about that?"

"Nothing magical, really. But by the way you keep fussing with that band, I can see that it's something you've acquired recently. How long ago did she present it to you?"

"I don't know. Three or four weeks, I guess."

"About the time you began quarreling with Mrs. Hartney, and just before the incident of the cats?"

He thought a moment. "Yes, I suppose that's right. But what of it? Are you suggesting that after the rows about Rona began with my wife, I took to exterminating cats to vent my hostilities? You really are reaching, aren't you?"

It's an investigator's lot to be abused. I wasn't provoked, I simply asked another question.

"Was the shed out back of here your usual place of meeting?"

"Yes."

"And was it normally kept locked?"

"Yes. But Rona had a key. I provided her with one."

"And was it her custom to be early, to arrive and let herself in before you got there yourself?"

"Generally, yes. What of it?"

"No particular reason, Mr. Hartney."

But I was thinking that when people have a habit of doing things, others can easily learn what those habits are -- and take advantage. I got up to go.

"How did you injure that hand, Mr. Hartney?"

The question stirred him up again, like fuel put to an open flame.

"I didn't hurt it stringing up Rona!" Tears glistened in his eyes. "I burnt it on my oven four days ago, all right? I had it seen to at the walk-in clinic just up the street -- a Doctor Mowett. I'm sure they keep really good records if you want to check up on me!"

Before leaving, I walked up the side of the shop, past the shed where the body had been found, to the lane that serviced the rear of the street. It was a narrow passage, with high fences and blank brick walls, almost a canyon. A place where anyone could move without notice, especially at night. I imagined the fences hung with dead cats and shuddered. Hartney was right about one thing -- any mind behind such deeds was decidedly warped.

But not as warped as the mind behind the killing of Miss Rona Cleary.

I bent my footsteps up the lane.

The Clearys occupied a small wartime house behind a high chain link fence, half a block down from the Hartneys. Unlike the Hartney home, it was very well kept, with window trim neatly painted, windows all in one piece, yard carefully tended and a large burgeoning garden. I found the Clearys out back staking tomato plants in black weeded earth.

They conducted me into the house, where Mrs. Cleary, a thin tiny woman, was able to make good her promise of tea. I chose my words carefully; it's always a delicate thing, discussing with parents the death of their child. It turned out that Mrs. Cleary was the communicative one; her husband sat stolidly silent in a corner with his brawny arms propped across his chest.

"I was shocked when she told me she was seeing a married man," Mrs. Cleary said with a damp sniff into a tissue which emerged in a crumpled wad from her sleeve.

"She told you that? She admitted it?"

"Oh, yes. She even showed me the key he had given her -- that was my Rona, honest to a fault. She never kept anything from me very long. Of course, I tried to talk her out of it. I told her that seeing a married man would only lead to grief. And then when John told me what a monster that Hartney'd been as a child -- John was custodian at the school then, you see." Mrs. Cleary shook her head and closed her eyes. "But I never dreamed anything like this would happen. If only she had listened."

I noted the consistent first person singular.

"Was it only in you that she confided, Mrs. Cleary? Not in your husband as well?" I looked at Cleary, who had not budged but sat as immovable as a tree stump, returning my gaze with eyes that were flat, unequivocal, and slightly disdainful.

"Well," said Mrs. Cleary, "naturally between Rona and I it was one woman to another. Female talk. You understand that. And John isn't -- wasn't her real father. I remarried when Rona was ten."

Cleary gave a curt nod at his wife, as if signalling that this was as much about the subject as I needed to know.

When I asked to see the daughter's room, Mrs. Cleary led me to it. I found it tidy, modestly but tastefully decorated with a few travel posters and some dried floral arrangements. I peered into the foot of the closet and saw several pairs of shoes, white ones, brown, and red. A few neatly pressed dresses hung above them. I followed Mrs. Cleary back to the living room.

"You've said Rona was open with you. Does that mean she told you the details of her relationship with Hartney? Where they met, and how often, all that sort of thing?"

"Oh, no. There were some things she kept to herself." Mrs. Cleary screwed up her face and began to cry again. This time her grief seemed a little forced. "I just can't believe my Rona's gone. I don't know why she ever took up with that horrible man. That murderer!"

I frowned at her.

"I'm not sure you ought to say that, Mrs. Cleary. Nobody has yet suggested murder here. A suicide is how we're officially viewing it."

"Then you're crazy! All of you. My husband worked at Hartney's school, so he knows. And Hartney did kill all those cats just weeks ago. Strung them up along the lane, choked to death." She was angry now, her own claws out. "I suppose a suicide would be convenient for you. A lot less work. But let me tell you, that Mr. Hartney is a crazy man. First he killed cats, and then he killed my daughter. It's as plain as the nose on your face." She had risen from her chair. "Get out of here, Mr. Smart Policeman. I won't talk to you anymore."

Mr. Cleary followed me out of the house, and determined to put the last of my questions, I asked, "About the way Rona was dressed the night she died, was it usual for her to go off to meet Hartney in those clothes?"

"All the time," Cleary growled. "That dress, those shoes -- I seen her go out like that plenty of times."

At the gate, I turned.

"You keep a fine-looking property, Mr. Cleary." I glanced about at the flowers and the closely-cropped lawn. The high steel-link fence looked brand new, and I noticed that the space between the bottom of the fence and the ground had been carefully lined with screen. I pointed. "Is that to keep rodents out of the garden?"

Cleary nodded, glowering. "That's what it's for, all right. A man works hard at his garden, he doesn't like the vermin creeping in to ruin it."

"Well," I said, "it's too bad about the cats then -- I imagine they did a lot to keep the vermin down."

Cleary's narrow eyes scrutinized me closely. Was it to detect frivolity?

Descending the sidewalk to my car, I reviewed the things I had learned. That Rona Cleary had been a bright young thing, direct, open and trusting, with a flare for the fine points of fashion. That her lover, Hartney, was henpecked, unsuccessful and un-happy. That Rona Cleary's mother was convinced that Hartney was their daughter's murderer. I suspected also that there was something not quite genuine about the Clearys, that Mrs. Cleary's final outburst had been more a calculated attempt to get rid of an interogator than an expression of genuine grief.

Not genuine...

I thought I had found out what might have given me that feeling when I got back to my desk and found the report sent up earlier by Central Registry. It did not bear the name of Cleary, but of Ransom, a now-deceased aunt of the ten-year-old Rona. This aunt had sworn out a complaint against Cleary for the physical abuse of his stepdaughter. The complaint had been dismissed at the time for lack of evidence, and the non-corroboration of Mrs. Cleary. The aunt, who had been elderly even then, had subsequently moved away and died a natural death.

I exited the building wanting a stroll to sort out my thoughts. The death of Rona Cleary looked now even less like a suicide. Had it been an act of violence by her lover, an admitted animal abuser? Or by her stepfather, who'd been all too ready to lay violent hands

on her earlier in life? Even Mrs. Hartney could be considered a
suspect -- she certainly had a motive. And if the death was a
murder, it meant a deliberately contrived scene of suicide had been
arranged. Why? Because the murderer was somebody who was
sure to fall under suspicion? Someone Rona knew? A stranger,
after all -- some violent transient who may have intercepted Rona
Cleary in the lane -- would scarcely have gone to such trouble. And
the fact that there were no signs of struggle on the body (she had
not been raped, there were no bruises or cuts) implied that her
assailant was someone with whom she was familiar.

Someone she knew, then -- but who?

Shadows moved on shadows at the back of my mind. Something about the shoes. I reached for the thought, almost grasped it,
but it flitted away.

The shop windows slipped by as I walked on with my mind
on those shoes, puzzling. A display of shoes caught my eye, and I
stopped to look in at them. There were many styles, among them
a pair that, although a different colour, were much like the shoes I
had found at the scene of the crime --

I caught myself up. A crime? Well, suicide was a crime of a
sort, too, after all. Looking at the shoes in the display caused a
question to rise in my mind, and on impulse I entered the shop to
question the clerk.

She was a thin, spectacled woman who reminded me of a
school-teacher. I led her over to the window display.

"These shoes here, do they come in other colours?"

"Yes, one other colour. They're available in black."

"May I see a black pair, please?"

Having anticipated a sale, she looked disappointed.

"I'm sorry. We only carry black in that style in the winter."

"And why is that?"

"Black is a winter colour for that particular shoe, sir. So if
you're considering a gift for someone, the white would be more
appreciated..."

I puzzled over that.

"Black, a winter colour?" I glanced round the shop, immediately spotted a pair of black shoes on the wall, and pointed. "What
about those?"

The clerk smiled.

"Those are patent leathers. One can wear patents in black in
the summertime. But they require the company of a matching
handbag or belt for style..."

The clerk's voice faded. I was thinking of Rona Cleary's body
hanging so very unstylishly in the midst of a rough shed. I saw her
white dress, her red belt, her black shoes. I realized that part of my
education had gone entirely lacking, a detective had to be
knowledgable of many things.

Winter shoes ... dark winter shoes with a red belt.

The clerk chattered a while on the subject of ladies shoes, and when her lecture was done, I summarized, "So a lady does not wear dark shoes in that style in the summer, unless they are patent leather, and she ought not to wear shoes that conflict with her purse or belt. Is that correct?"

The clerk nodded, a faint smile on her lips. She seemed pleased. She had sold nothing but she'd had an apt pupil.

Back at my desk, I took out the lab report and re-read it. One of the questions in my mind was whether Rona Cleary might have been strangled elsewhere, then her body removed to the shed to give the appearance of suicide. But the report did not suggest this. The twine had cut deep into the flesh of the neck, leaving only the welts of the makeshift noose (there were no other marks), and the medical examiner reported that the observed effects of hemor-rhaged eyeballs and protruding tongue could only have been pro-duced on a living body.

Then I noted a telling detail: thick, short cotton fibers had been found on the body as well -- the sort that might have been shed by a terry cloth towel: it was likely the girl had taken a bath or a shower shortly before her death.

I collected the keys to Hartney's shed, which had been locked up tight since the body had been found, and drove to the scene armed with a tape measure and Rona Cleary's black shoes. Shut up for days under a hot June sun, the shed was stuffy and hot.

I first positioned the stool under the rafter where the body had been suspended. I then set the shoes upright on the stool, feeling a twinge as I placed them just where the small dangling feet had once been. Next I measured downward from the flat of the beam the seventy-one inches noted in the crime lab report. The problem was evident immediately: even with the high-heeled shoes in position, the feet would have to have been floating a good two inches above them in the air!

The observation sobered me. I had been almost ready to entertain the unlikelihood that Miss Cleary had first stood on the tops of her buckled shoes, then when the noose was tied, kicked them away, so that they fell by some odd chance in neat formation.

But the evidence was plain: no suicide this!

I let myself out of the shed and carefully locked the door. There was someone I wanted to interview again, someone whom I hoped might provide me a deeper insight...

Overdale broke off his narrative, glancing up. "...and so I drove slowly and thoughtfully downtown and into the manufacturing district." He stared at Wilde. "So what have you got so far? What would you have done next under the circumstances I've de-scribed?"

"Let me think on it," Wilde replied. He had consumed his ice cream down to the last inch of cone, and now he popped the remaining delicious morsel into his mouth and munched it. He opened one hand and began striking off points on his fingers. "A death by hanging. A lover with an injured hand and a history of animal cruelty. A bizarre attack on the local cat population. An ill-tempered, jealous wife, protective of her husband. A vindictive mother, and a sulking stepfather who may have mistreated the victim as a child..."

"And who happens to be a gardener," Overdale put in.

Wilde looked sharply at him.

"Right, a gardener, though I don't see what that signifies. Gardeners are a gentle bunch, aren't they? Primping the tendrils of plants and dusting for bugs." He thought a long moment, then offered, "I'll tell you this much -- since you proved that it had to be murder, only one of the principals can be ruled out, and that's Mrs. Cleary, who was physically too small. Both Mr. Cleary and Hartney had the strength -- and maybe even Mrs. Hartney, whom you've described as a 'tank'. Any one of them could have done the job. Cleary out of anger; he'd showed violence towards the girl earlier on, and he might have viewed Hartney as a competitor of some sort -- his feelings for his stepdaughter may not have been sexually healthy. Mrs. Hartney out of jealousy. Hartney himself out of fear for his marriage -- maybe he tried to break the relationship off and the girl threatened to embarrass him. Any one of those three."

"And the circumstances? Take Mr. Cleary..."

"Easy. He follows his stepdaughter to her rendezvous with Hartney, breaks in on her before Hartney arrives, and when she won't return home with him, in a fit of rage -- the sort of rage we know he was capable of -- he strangles her and leaves the body in the shed hoping to implicate Hartney --"

Overdale interrupted brusquely.

"No, that won't do. Why then hang the body from a rafter? Better to leave it sprawled on the floor. And aren't you forgetting something about the shoes?"

"What, in particular?"

"Why were they not a matching part of Rona Cleary's outfit? Remember my lesson at the shoe store: how could a fashion conscious young lady like Rona Cleary go off to meet her lover wearing the wrong shoes? Fashionable girl's don't wear dull black leather with red patent belts."

Wilde made a face. Overdale continued, "And you haven't even offered to explain the cats."

"The cats," Wilde said with an air of wounded authority, "are a red herring you threw in to create confusion."

"I assure you they played a certain role."

"Humm. Well, I admit I don't have *all* the answers. I'll need more information to work the details out."

"And so did I," said Overdale. "As I was saying, I had arranged another interview..."

Mrs. Hartney arrived at the restaurant looking harried and somewhat out of place. As she hastened toward my table at the direction of the hostess, I almost wished I had chosen more simple surroundings -- perhaps a pub.

She bustled up, breathless, and stopped in the aisle.

"Mr. Overdale?"

She seemed to be avoiding my official title purposely.

She wore a tatty raincoat, too heavy for the heat. Her broad strong hands gripped her purse as if she were afraid somebody would snatch it away from her. Her eyes were small, unaccentuated with makeup, and they studied me with distrust.

I rose and pulled out a chair.

"I hope, Mrs. Hartney, this restaurant suits you. I tried to get you at home several times, but you always seem to be working. The alternative was to come and speak with you at your place of work, and I prefer to avoid that if I can."

"I'll put up with the place." We might have been discussing a punishment. She seated herself heavily, refusing to give up her coat. "I only get forty-five minutes for lunch so you better be quick."

"As quick as I can, Mrs. Hartney."

"I hope these waiters are fast off the hop."

"I'm sure they are."

"Good help's hard to get. I should know, owning a bakery, my husband and me."

Perhaps "bakery" was an exaggeration -- "bakeshop" might have described the Hartney operation more exactly.

"That brings up a question, Mrs. Hartney. Why do you work downtown instead of helping out your husband in the shop?"

Her sharp gaze narrowed.

"You know the answer to that already, don't you? You police always know the answer before asking the question. It's part of your training. Don't try to fool me. I read mysteries -- those Charlie Salter stories." I remembered the paperbacks in the Hartney apartment. "Never mind, I'll answer you anyway. It's because we don't get along. Two hours in a hot room together and we're ready to make each other into pies. So I leave the bakery to him. Business is slow, and he can run things himself. He starts the ovens at five, gets through baking by ten, and then he just has to open the doors and mind the till. He likes it that way, and he's welcome to it. I'm happier down here."

I remarked her scowl-lined face; she did not look happy. Remembering the dingy rooms, I said, "I take it, Mrs. Hartney, that the bakery is not doing well."

She snorted. "That's a polite way of putting it."

"It indicates to me that your husband has time on his hands."

"What's that supposed to mean?" The waiter came, took down her order of tossed salad and soup, then hurried away. "You're saying that's what got him into trouble with that young slut, aren't you? That he chased after her, that he was the aggressive one. That's what you're driving at."

I shrugged. "It had crossed my mind."

"Well, get it out of your mind. My husband had nothing to do with that situation."

"Really, Mrs. Hartney, he must share some of --"

"He don't share nothing. No flies on him at all. That Rona seduced him, plain and simple. You should see how them young harlots come into the shop, flaunting themselves. Clothes thin as nightshirts. Faces painted up like -- like *floozies*. That's an old word, I know, Mr. Overdale, but it fits, let me tell you. If you ever want to know what a 'floozie' is, come down to our shop one day and I'll show you one. Young girls today have no idea how to dress -- everything they wear is all wrong. Half-nude, most of them. And after all, my husband is only human, isn't he?"

She stopped to drink from her water glass, and I caught a glimpse of a stout wrist under her sleeve. A powerful woman. But was she strong enough to have pulled Rona Cleary so high up off her feet?

"Maybe we could talk," I said, " about the cats."

Our food arrived. Mrs. Hartney poked angrily at her salad as if there was something hidden in the greenery which she was determined to find.

"That talk about cats was all lies," she said as the waiter moved off. "All lies. My husband is fond of animals, he would never hurt one of God's little creatures."

And what of God's bigger creatures? What of a human being? What were his sentiments there? I wanted to ask.

"I mention it," I continued, "because it looks very bad for your husband at the moment. You must see that the evidence against him is harsh."

"No, I don't see it!" She javelined a pickle with her fork, withdrew the instrument and stabbed once again, viciously. "It's the craziest notion I ever heard, suspecting my husband of ... of such a thing. How could he manage it with an injured hand, anyways? And even if he could, do you think he would murder someone and then leave the body there on his own property to be found? He's no fool, you know. He's lazy and he's weak, but he's a clever man, my husband."

She leaned across the table, her salad forgotten.

"If you want to know who really killed those cats, go ask John Cleary why he built that tall fence around his yard a week or two ago -- a steel one that cats can't climb. And ask him what he did about cats before he had that fence. *I saw* what he did, one day when I was walking up the lane from the bus stop. He didn't hear me, didn't look up, but I saw him fooling with some old Coke box in his garden. Only it didn't look much like a Coke box anymore. He'd done something to it, put some kind of sacking and door on it. Later on I figured it out. He'd made that Coke box into a *trap!*"

I grew interested. "But if you knew this, why didn't you speak up about it at the time?"

"Because I was mad at my husband. I knew he was fooling with that tramp. Maybe I could have looked the other way, too. But he was shameless, taking to wearing the jewelry she'd given him openly in the house. Maybe I thought he deserved a little come-uppance right about then. I knew he couldn't have gotten into any *real* trouble."

"But now that he's under graver suspicion you've decided to come forward with this testimony about the trap?"

She nodded.

"I know the talk Mrs. Cleary's been spreading about my husband's school days, *and* I know where she got it from. And I know she's trying to make it look like he went from killing cats to killing people. But he had nothing to do with those strangled cats, and she knows it. Her own husband is a far more likely culprit. Mrs. Cleary won't face it but the fact is her daughter Rona committed suicide, and did it out of guilt! There was no murder!"

"You're convinced of that?"

"Of course. Why was the body hung up if it wasn't suicide? Murderers don't often use *that* method, even I know that. I read mysteries. And what about the shoes, eh? Why were they so carefully removed and set by on the floor? Because Rona Cleary took them off herself, it's the only possible explanation --"

She stopped, perhaps sensing that I was regarding her with a new and more critical interest.

"How did you know that fact about the shoes?" I asked.

She shifted in her chair, eyes sharp with resentment.

"My husband must have told me," she replied. She looked at her watch. "I got to get back. I'm late already. Or do you want to make me lose my job on top of everything else?"

With some admiration I watched her storm away between the tables, glaring other customers out of her path as if they had been placed there to obstruct her by a hostile management, a tough little woman, contemptuous of her husband but ready to defend him with the spirit of a lioness.

Then I thought again of Rona Cleary's black shoes. I thought about the cats and her stepfather's homemade trap. I thought about the twine. And I thought I knew what had happened in Hartney's rude shed that terrible night.

Leaving some money on the table, I went out after Mrs. Hartney.

She was easy to follow, a squat purposeful figure with her purse in her hand like a weapon.

In a ten minute walk she led me to a squalid stone building whose dreary lettering identified it unimaginatively as the Northway Clothing Mills. I followed her through the door, and along a dark aisle to her station. I recognised it as the receiving room. I watched her shrug off her coat and begin shifting ponderous rolls of cloth out of boxes and into tiered storage. She was strong. Very strong. I would have had trouble doing her job and I was half again her weight. As she heaved one heavy box after another up onto the second tier of a bin, I approached her quietly. I had decided an abrupt confrontation would be best.

"I think, Mrs. Hartney, that you must have done what you did in order to protect your husband. Am I right about that?"

She turned, gaping, her thick hand clutching the heavy chain of a hoist for support. I went on calmly, "You said your husband told you about the shoes. But in fact he did not remember a thing about them when I questioned him just hours after finding the body. So I find myself wondering how he could have told you the manner in which they were placed."

Her face clouded as though a storm were gathering there, and then just as suddenly her features went heavy and she seemed to sag against the chain.

"You know, then? You know what happened, what I had to do?"

I nodded. "Yes, I think so. But maybe things aren't as bad as you suppose. Will you accompany me now?"

"I brought her back to the office then," Overdale said, "and I took down her statement."

Wilde found himself sitting solidly in his seat, hands tented before him, brow furrowed with consternation. He was wondering if Overdale had not deliberately misled him.

"But if you're going to tell me after all this that Mrs. Hartney murdered the girl --"

"I'm not going to tell you that. In fact I'm going to tell you that she did nothing of the kind. She was simply trying to protect her husband."

"What? You're saying Hartney did it, then, sore hand and all?"

"No, I'm not saying that, either."

Wilde smacked the bench seat, scowling. "Then, damn it all, what are you saying?"

"I'm saying that I, a young detective, learned a valuable lesson from that case, that at a scene of violence things are rarely what they seem to be, and that the people involved in that violence can introduce no end of complications to the observable facts. As an old

investigator yourself, you wouldn't argue with that, would you?
Going back to the question of the cats..."

"Damn the cats! I told you the cats are a crock."

"And I told you they had a bearing. You've got to see them in
conjunction with Cleary's occupation as a gardener. He hated cats.
They were anathema to him. He as much as told me so. Mrs.
Hartney said she once saw him with a homemade trap, and I
believed her. He erected an expensive fence to keep them out of his
yard. But the fence was a last resort against cats; he had already
tried another means of dealing with them."

"Then he *was* the one who --"

"Precisely. He trapped them one at a time, throttled them
with twine he'd collected over the months from Hartney's store
and hung them along the lane as a warning to the good folk of the
neighbourhood to keep their pets at home. It didn't work, cats being
the independent creatures that they are, and so he built the fence.
But he learned something from his efforts. The effect of his wife's
slanderous attack upon Hartney must have impressed him deeply.
Still, I doubt he planned anything. He killed the cats not as part of
a plot to discredit Hartney -- I don't think he was capable of such
convoluted scheming -- but simply because he hated the creatures.
Then, as circumstances played into his hands he took advantage of
them. He may not have been smart, but he was sly."

"Fine. Damn the cats." Wilde rubbed his hands together.
"Let's get back to the murder. Who really did kill Rona Cleary?"

Overdale grinned devilishly. "You haven't figured that out?"

"I thought I had before when I suggested Cleary did it. You
talked me out of that. Now you've dragged Mrs. Hartney into it,
saying you took her back to your office and charged her -- you've
muddied it all up again."

"Kindly pay attention. I didn't say I charged her, I said I took
her statement."

"But what had she *done*?"

"She'd killed Rona Cleary."

Wilde felt himself turning purple. "But, *damn* it all, Overdale
--"

Overdale held out his hand in a calming gesture, stretched his
legs and crossed his hands over his stomach.

"Listen. You see, Mrs. Hartney also knew of the arrangements usually followed by the two lovers. She had gone down to
the shed to remonstrate with Rona Cleary, and letting herself in
only moments after the murderer had gone, found the body
sprawled on the floor. She mistakenly assumed that her husband
was responsible, and in her cold but methodical manner she set
about doing what she could to protect him. She did not realize that
the poor girl was still alive!" He sighed. "Criminal negligence -- a
manslaughter charge was dropped -- and obstructing the police. It

was she who arranged the body to make it appear like a suicide. And a good job she made of it, too. She fooled me."

"You were a rookie," Wilde reminded him flatly, "anything would have fooled you. So there was no murderer -- are you going to tell me who the attacker was, or not?"

Overdale pouted, feigning disappointment.

"Aren't you supposed to guess? I've done all the work for you."

Wilde said, "Well, if it wasn't Hartney, and if it wasn't Mrs. Hartney, then it could only have been -- Cleary!"

"Bingo."

Wilde was both pleased and annoyed at once. "That's just what I said in the first place. It was your questioning me why he'd have bothered staging the suicide that put me off the scent. All right, so you helped me a little with the solution. What brought *you* round to suspecting that Cleary was responsible?"

"The shoes. The fact that they didn't match the victim's outfit. She would never have left her house in shoes like that. Which means somebody took her out of the house, either dead or unconscious, and brought the shoes along as an afterthought. That someone, I reasoned, had to have been either Mr. or Mrs. Cleary, and Mrs. Cleary would have known what shoes to take.

"I think Cleary confronted his daughter at the house while she was dressing, and she had a towel draped round her neck to protect her clothes while she put on her makeup. He knew where she was off to and he forbade her to go. They quarreled, he became violent, took hold of the towel and throttled her, the thick pile leaving no mark. He must have thought he'd killed her, though she was only unconscious. The key gave him an idea. He carried her to the shed -- a minimal risk, just a few dozen yards to go. He brought a pair of shoes along from the bottom of her closet; they were the wrong colour and style, but that meant nothing to him. He threw them helter-skelter in the shed. Then remembering the cats and hoping to frame Hartney, he snatched down a length of the twine that hung in loops on the wall, twisted one end of it tight around her neck and left, certain that Hartney would be blamed."

Wilde frowned up, displeased with himself.

"His ploy might have worked too," Overdale continued, "but he didn't anticipate Mrs. Hartney being first on the scene. She arranged the shoes neatly, doubled up the twine into a rope and raised the body under the beam. She admitted to me later that she saw that the shoes and the belt didn't match, but thought nothing of it, being of the opinion that young girls don't know how to dress. She wasn't aware that Rona Cleary was an exception to her rule."

"Mrs. Hartney's trickery, then, was superimposed upon Cleary's. A double confusion."

"Yes. If I had come upon things as Cleary had left them, the scene of a murder, my blood might have been up. I might have ruled out Hartney because of his hand, but I doubt that I would have noticed that the shoes were wrong. Cleary might have gone Scott free. As things stood, though, suicide was believable. At least until Mrs. Cleary railed against it and started me thinking about the shoes."

"Did you get a confession out of Cleary?"

"Yes, though it mightn't have been that simple without the Dragon Lady's help. When she heard the questions I was putting to her husband, she started right in on him. He broke about five minutes later. I told you she was the type who could handle him."

They rose to go, Wilde brushing a wafer crumb from his slacks.

"Strange that Cleary wasn't observant enough to take the proper shoes along that night -- shoes that would have matched his daughter's outfit."

"Yes, well, he was an ignorant brute," Overdale replied. "Imagine a man living for years with a woman and not knowing the simplest thing about her manner of dress."

"Yes," said Wilde, "imagine it."

The two old bachelors strode off towards home.

William Bankier

William Bankier grew up in Belleville and now
lives in Los Angeles. He worked as a hotel
bellboy and desk clerk, a radio DJ, and an ad
writer before turning to fiction full time. His first
mystery story, "It Happened in Act One",
appeared in *Ellery Queen's Mystery Magazine*
in July 1962. Since then, he's sold dozens,
including his Edgar Award nominated "The
Choirboy" in 1980. In 1989, Bankier's "One
Day at a Time" was shortlisted for the Crime
Writers of Canada's Arthur Ellis Award for Short
Fiction. Among Bankier's most popular work are
the Baytown stories, set in a fictionalized
Belleville. They range from near farce to dark
tragedy, and most often deal with the destructive
potential of the failed marriage and the family
perverted by greed and suspicion. "One More
Story To Tell" is a tale of suspense rising from
just such a situation. It's classic Bankier.

ONE MORE STORY TO TELL

by William Bankier

So once upon a time in Ontario, in a place called Baytown, there was a middle-aged writer who sold never more than four short stories a year to American magazines. His name was Bernard Heft and he worked on the desk at the Coronet Hotel because the income from his story sales did not meet his expenses. It hardly paid the taxes on the cottage he had inherited six years ago when his father died. Heft and his sister Pauline, who had left her husband in Toronto and had come home to look after her big brother, got on quite well.

"Crokinole?" he would ask her when the table was cleared, the dishes done and the television listing weighed and found wanting.

"Why not?" Pauline would drag out the board from under the china cabinet and place it on the dining room table. Heft would take down his pewter tankard and spill from it the two dozen wooden roundels -- 12 black, 12 red. Then they would play for an hour, flicking the roundels accurately across the polished surface with a practiced snap of index finger and thumb, knocking an opposing piece off the board while leaving the attacking roundel in its place. Satisfying. Especially since the game was so out-of-date nobody they spoke to about it had even heard the name, let alone knew how to play.

"What gives tomorrow?" Pauline would say when they were closing windows and turning off lights.

"Finishing a story, I hope. I'll have a chance to work at the hotel. Danforth asked if I could do the night shift."

"Boo. It's lonely around here with you gone all night and then sleeping the next day."

"It's extra money, kid."

From dark rooms on either side of the hall at the head of the stairs, brother and sister would sustain the ritual of a lifetime. "Night, Paulie!" "Night, Bernie!" Then silence, with only the cistern in the bathroom whispering intermittently where a valve wanted adjusting.

The appearance on tour in Baytown of an English drama group, the Hartfield Players, should not have turned upside down the comfortable lives of Bernard and Pauline Heft, but it did. It did because of the beauty and talent of Olivia Darkling. And she was not even British or one of the actors. She was the business manager, a quick-witted, street-talking New Yorker with perfect lips and dusky, middle-eastern eyes assessing the world across tartar cheekbones.

"Keep tabs on the trashy show-folk," Jack Danforth said to Heft behind the desk one afternoon when the group had been in town for a week, doing a season of Pinter and Ayckbourn at the high school auditorium.

"They paid a good deposit when they checked in." Heft was not yet aware that he had fallen in love with Olivia Darkling. She had just dropped off her key and gone out of the hotel to the measured tap of expensive heels.

Danforth stared at the screen door which was still swinging behind her. "Yes, but the account is rising. They're charging a lot of their meals." He shifted two inches of dead cigar. "Trashy show-folk," he concluded.

And it came to pass that the Hartfield Players fell afoul of economic reality. But they did not attempt a moonlight flit as the cynical hotel-owner had implied. When their run was ended, Olivia Darkling came to the desk with all the keys. The cast members were loading baggage and themselves into their raunchy station-wagon which, Heft was noticing through the lobby window, had one whitewall tire and the back door wired shut. "I'd like a word with the manager, please," she said. The dark eyes penetrated Heft's, reading his response although he was not the man she had to persuade.

"Will you be okay, Olivia?" The leading actor, a Tyrone Power look-alike in his late twenties, came up behind her and put his hands on her shoulders. His name was Morris Carrington. "I can stay with you."

"No, you go on with the others. You can't miss Australia, that role is once in a lifetime."

Carrington kissed her and went away and Bernard Heft led the woman through to Danforth's back office. Then he lingered in the doorway to the lounge where he could overhear the gist of the conversation.

"I do appreciate your levelling with me," the manager said at one point. "But the account represents a lot of money."

"Which I consider to be *my* debt to the hotel. I organized this tour, not the Hartfield. The error is mine. And I intend to make it good."

"Post-dated checks are not..."

"No checks. A series of lectures. Hear me out, sir. Your back lounge seats at least fifty. You sell alcohol from the bar. On successive nights for as long as it takes, we advertise 'On the Road In Britain and Canada' with the world-famous theatrical impres-sario Olivia Darkling. That's a bit excessive, but ..."

"I like it," Danforth said and, out in the lounge, Heft knew this exceptional woman had brought it off. And she was going to be around for a while.

By the time the lectures were history and the outstanding debt had been worked off, Olivia Darkling was very much *persona grata* in Baytown. Heft, who took some of his meals in the Coronet dining room, sat with her at a small table by the window on the day Danforth receipted the Hartfield account and handed it to her with a shy flourish. "What happens now?" the desk clerk asked her. "Will you rejoin the players?"

"No, they've scattered to the four winds. Actors are tumble-weed. Morris Carrington, for example, is probably in Sydney by now, starting on a series for Australian TV."

"Back to New York, then?"

"Possibly. I'm wide open." Her eyes went from brilliant to devastating as she turned loose some amusement on the helpless man facing her. "I'm waiting for the next episode in the soap opera of my life."

What Heft wanted to say was, "Please don't leave." The words were so close to being spoken, he felt she ought to be able to hear them. Perhaps she did because she went on to say,

"I love this town. What a change from New York."

Perversely, he flirted with disappointment. "You must miss the big city buzz."

"Yes, but I'm ready for a change."

"Then you could stay here." He was in. The water was fine. "I don't mean the hotel. My house. I'm a writer, not just a hotel clerk. I need help. You could edit my stories, tell me where they fall down. I know you'd be good, you've got brains in large amounts. There's lots of room. You'd have no expenses. I'd pay you for your help..."

"Bernard," she said, putting a hand over his, stopping his heart as she halted his pitch. "May I call you Bernard? You don't have to sell me."

He was afraid to smile, the whole dining room would see his face and they would know. Soberly, he assured her, "It'll be okay. My sister lives there."

Pauline Heft hated the new arrangement. But it was Bernie's house and he was out of his mind so there was nothing she could do but frown and bear it.

"You could be a little more gracious," he told her after three months. Olivia was at the library researching a detail she thought was incorrect in Heft's latest manuscript. "She's trying hard."

"With you."

"Bitchy, Pauline."

"You should hear her with me when you're not in the house. You've never seen the real Olivia."

"Or maybe you bring out the worst in her."

"Three's a crowd, Bern. Isn't that the point?"

"You said it. Paulie. Not me."

But Pauline Heft stayed put -- where could she go? To relocate in Baytown would make her look insane. Toronto could only offer the husband she no longer wanted. "Maybe you'll come to your senses," she sighed. "My big brother *is* almost fifty years old."

Heft turned fifty. Olivia put down some roots. Pauline told herself things could be worse; at least they were not sleeping with each other. She knew Bernie. If the gypsy ever once got into his bed it would mean marriage, kids, the lot. And Pauline would have no choice but to go back to Toronto and take a deep breath while trying to remember her husband's redeeming features.

Then the major development took place -- Olivia began telling her stories.

The first one happened by accident. It was Thanksgiving weekend. With traditional sentiments conquering jealousy, the women cooperated in the kitchen to produce a feast. There was turkey with sausage stuffing, chutneyed peach halves, crab apples in cinnamon syrup, mashed potatoes, brussels sprouts, bushels of tossed salad and a succulent pumpkin pie. Bernie opened a third bottle of wine and they ended up staring into the fire through snifters of Courvoisier.

Perhaps Olivia picked her time. In any case, Pauline had gone to bed when the New Yorker began to recall the adventure of a young widow who lived in a converted loft and wrote poetry and the cop who came around one night to investigate a robbery, and the dog on the fire escape, and the widow's notebook containing her most intimate thoughts which fell five floors, landing on the roof of the squad car. The story contained interesting characters, pathos, humor ... and Olivia told it well.

When she was finished, Heft said almost enviously, "I could do something with that. Mind if I try?"

"Be my guest. I've got a million of them."

"A thousand and one, anyway," he told her, leaning across the sofa and kissing her between the caravan eyes. "My own Scheherazade!"

He spent the next few days with notebook and then with typewriter and when he was finished, he showed the manuscript to its originator. She read it and said, "Don't change a thing."

Heft mailed the story to his agent who sold it within the month to a quality magazine for a fee three times what he was usually paid. To Olivia, he said, "This could be the start of something big." And when the check came through, he bought her a jade ring she had been admiring. Pauline froze when she saw the ring so he gave his sister the price of a holiday in Toronto. "Run into Peter?" he asked her when she got back.

"Why should I have seen him?" she retorted. "I live here. Sorry."

And so the relationship developed with an armed truce existing between the women and Bernard in the middle, enjoying (truth be told) his position as the dominant person in both their lives.

The second story emerged in cold blood, so to speak. No dinner, no wine, no fireside magic. The writer simply went to his source and asked her, please, to do it again. She sat with her legs crossed on the sofa in the room where he did his work and let her eyes wander. "There was this couple who did back-stage duties at a theater off-off-Broadway. Eloise and Peggy. Eloise had been trying to get somebody to read a play she had been writing, it seemed, forever..."

Bernie scribbled while Olivia talked and a month later, the story was sold to the same magazine for half as much again as the first one. It simply worked. The material of Olivia Darkling's life in the city, which included the experiences of countless friends, could apparently be shaped by this small-town author into stories which were purchased eagerly by the editors of several class publications.

And not just editors. An independent film producer, three years into the informal collaboration, approached Bernard Heft's agent and paid a hundred thousand dollars for the motion picture rights to the story about the lonely poet and the cop. Then, with surprising efficiency, he went ahead and made the film, putting Heft down for 2% of the gross. And the film was a smash. And Heft woke up one day, four years into his astonishing affair with the gypsy raconteuse, to a realisation that never again would he have money problems. Only tax problems.

It was the fact that her brother had begun sleeping with the beautiful bitch that got so far up Pauline Heft's nose she could no longer breathe. "Are you two going into the baby business?" she said to Bernie late one morning when Olivia, bathed and glowing, had taken a basket over her arm and gone drifting gently away from the house in the direction of the market square.

Heft laughed at the suggestion. "We're crazy about each other, Paulie. Not plain crazy. I'm 54, she's 36. Not a good age to be begetting. No, we're making sure we don't get pregnant. If it should happen, it'll be a quick abortion. We've discussed it." But the writer could not ignore the pang of regret he felt when he spoke of denying life to the child he wanted more than all the splendid stories he might yet create.

"Have you any idea how ridiculous you look to our friends?"

"I'd like to know. I might be able to use the material."

"I never thought I'd live to see it."

"Unfortunately," Heft said, "you have." He took notebook and pen off the kitchen table and performed his disapproving walk towards the study door. "Maybe it's time for the one-way ticket to Toronto. I'll be glad to pay."

Something Pauline never did was disturb her big brother while he was writing. She did so half an hour later, going to the oak door, giving it one ugly thump and then flinging it open so he could see the suitcase in her hand and the rage on her face. "Okay, I'm off. See you some time."

"Bon voyage."

"You really will be sorry. That woman is not a Baytown person."

"Nor, perhaps, am I. She makes me happy, Paulie. Sorry about that. And she's lifted my work. Too bad I can't remain a third-rate stick-in-the-mud so you would not feel so threatened."

Pauline blinked. She started to speak three times but no words came. Tears came instead. Bernie made parallel lines with his pen under the last word he had written. At last she turned and walked away leaving his door open -- a thing she had never done. Moments later she was back, minus the suitcase which was resting now, and would remain for months, at the foot of the stairs.

"Why should *I* leave?" she said with more composure than her brother had heard out of her in years. "I live here. Let *her* leave."

Heft did not travel to Hollywood for the Academy Award presentations. A famous scenarist was receiving the Oscar for best screenplay which he had based on the poet/cop story. Heft watched the TV coverage with Olivia on the sofa beside him and Pauline getting out of her chair and leaving the room every few minutes as if she was an alcoholic and her flask was in her coat.

"You should be up there," Olivia said as the statuette was handed to a glittering young man in immaculate evening dress but with his tie undone.

"My agent says we've got a film offer on another story."

"You're brilliant."

"Thanks to you."

The telephone rang (not for the first time; friends had been calling up to say congratulations) and Pauline answered in the other room. Then she stuck her head through the doorway and said, without looking at the couple on the sofa, "No need to answer this one. It's Jack Danforth from the Coronet. Wants you to come in tomorrow and do the night shift."

Although he no longer needed the money, Heft continued to work on the hotel desk. Partly it was loyalty and a wish not to appear snobbish. Partly, he got a kick out of the contact with a lot of different people. Perhaps most important was a superstitious feeling that things were working and if anything changed, he might dry up. "Tell him okay," he said.

"I already did."

It was a quiet night on the Coronet desk. By midnight, nobody was coming or going so Heft began seven hours of uninterrupted solitude, the monotony broken only by his trips upstairs to check for smoke and his occasional expedition into the kitchen to cut a massive slice of cherry pie and pour a tankard of cold milk.

At two o'clock, he rang home because he was lonely. Olivia always stayed up late when he was out of the house and was available for consultations. But Pauline answered tonight with a lilt in her voice which Heft thought was a mixture of despondency and something strange he could not identify. After saying Olivia was not around -- okay, she sometimes got restless and hit the road in the new Porsche -- Pauline let hang a few seconds of silence and then said, "Would it surprise you, brother of mine, if I told you I love you?"

"Been hitting the vodka?"

"Thanks for your sensitive response. You can't change me, Bernie. I am what I am. And I love you more than you will even understand."

"Paulie," he said, a few seconds too late, "I love you, too."

"Sometimes," she concluded just before she rang off, "I surprise myself. I am the fool of all time."

In the morning, seedy from lack of sleep and bloated with a full-course Coronet breakfast, Heft arrived home to discover his sister was gone. The packed bag was no longer at the foot of the stairs.

"Did she say anything?" he asked Olivia.

"I didn't see her go. I was cruising across the Bay, I must have covered half of the county. When I got back, she wasn't here."

Heft's face went vacant. He began to sing in a funky voice a bit like Jose Feliciano: "Goin' to Toronto, baby but I can't take you..." Neither his heart nor his mind were in it. "Damn," he said. "I'm going to miss her."

Olivia put her arms around his waist and hugged him hard. "Darling," she said in a persuasive tone, "we'll be happier just the two of us."

In the mirror behind the china cabinet, he could see she was looking intently at herself as she hugged him. "True," he said. "It's what we wanted."

He tried to sleep but could not. Strange. After working all night, he should have crashed for eight hours. Could the departure of old Paulie with her blatant jealousy upset his equilibrium this much? He got up to go to the bathroom, came back with a glass of water, stood drinking it at the bedroom window. The sight of the garden always soothed him. The cross-shaped lawn dividing the planted areas into four rectangles. the sundial dead center. The bird-house on its crooked pole by the back fence. The red peonies. The iris, blue and yellow. His father had filled every square foot with floral beauty. The hydrangea, the clump of honeysuckle and ...

Heft focussed on a strip of freshly-turned earth. Extending along the near side of the farthest quadrant, it looked to be about six feet long by two feet wide. The dark soil seemed naked; it appeared obscene in the midst of so many growing things.

"Can't sleep?" Olivia was in the doorway behind him. She walked quietly to his side, looked where he was looking. "I got rid of all that clover," she said. "I told you I was going to clean it out."

"Looks good."

"I was full of energy all night. I went out and did it at dawn. I had to *do* something." Again, both arms went about his waist. "I'm going to put in sunflowers."

She tucked him into bed, lay down beside him, caressed him. He slept, but not for long. When he jolted awake, the light in the room was unchanged and Olivia was sitting in the window seat, looking out and down. He stared at her cameo profile, waiting for her to register the fact that he was watching her. At last, he had to speak.

"Is something wrong?"

She was not startled. "I want life to be simple," she said.

"And?"

"It isn't. It's like the stories I tell you. They are mostly the truth, by the way. Some embellishments. I would like us to be left alone. We get on well. It's peaceful in Baytown."

"You go mad. You drive all night."

"Only when you aren't here. And driving soothes me, it's harmless."

"Well," he said, "Paulie has left us alone. We should be happy."

She changed positions in the window seat, gave him the full sad weight of her expression. "You think it's that easy?"

In the following weeks Heft got in some useful hours at the typewriter. Olivia had told him a long story about an immigrant waiter at a New York restaurant who made so much money in tips that he owned an apartment building. But his young wife was into drugs -- and so were the men who came around. There was enough material that Heft was trying to shape it into a novella.

As for his companion, she broached the idea of a trip to Europe by sea. With money no problem, they could devote a couple of months to England, France, Italy. Heft had no objection. He gave her carte blanche and she began spending time with a travel agent, coming home with her handbag stuffed with brochures.

She also found time to plant sunflower seeds. They sprouted with vigor, producing plants two feet high within weeks and soon in need of staking. When he looked out at the six-foot patch from his window, Heft could never dispel the bad feelings. It was a preposterous assumption, but Pauline had done her vanishing act and the earth had been turned in the same night. All he had to do, of course, was telephone friends in Toronto to establish his sister was alive. But that might be embarrassing, especially since he did not want to talk to her. And if she was dead -- and Olivia had killed her -- dammit, he did not want to know!

Almost two months had passed since Pauline's departure when Olivia said to Bernard during breakfast, "Darling, I'm pregnant."

His heart lifted with joy, he could not conceal it. "Hey!"

"Remember what we agreed." The dark eyes were pools of some precious fluid. "At our ages, dearest. All kinds of problems. I'm going to have this terminated, pronto."

"What doctor will you see? In Baytown, there are no secrets."

"Poor man, I never meant to embarrass you socially." She got up from the table and carried her dishes to the sink. She rinsed each one carefully, studying the running water. Then she came back to the table and stood behind Heft's chair, placing her hands on his shoulders. "I know a good doctor in New York. I'll have it attended to there."

He felt fear verging on panic. Her stories were always explicit, every action and feeling described at length. But their personal communication took place on an instinctive level; not much was said. "Wish you well," he told her.

"Thanks."

He finished his coffee. "What will you do after?"

"I'm not sure."

His turn to get up. He went to the kitchen doorway. "You're never coming back," he said.

"I'm not sure," she repeated, but she glanced down.

"What we have here is so sweet." He inclined his head to indicate the house, their world. "I don't understand you."

On the eve of her departure for New York, they dressed up and went to dinner, rumbling across the bay bridge in the alien Porsche, turning heads at the County Gardens when they walked in with a reservation, she in salmon silk which was dance-floor length, he in his tuxedo, the only couple in the place so attired.

Home again at midnight, floating on wine, they brewed coffee and settled down on the sofa to extend their final evening together.

"One more story?" she suggested.

"Do I need it?" He felt as if he would never write again.

"We all need stories," she said. Tucking up her legs and

staring into an invisible campfire, she began, "Once upon a time, there was a man who lived in a village, in a fine cottage, with a good woman who was his sister." Using all her verbal skills, Olivia drew a word picture of life in the cottage and the harmony that existed there.

"Then, one day, a woman from the city arrived and found herself in difficulty. The brother took pity on her and invited the stranger into his house and into his life. They were happy -- but at the expense of the sister's peace of mind. She felt she had lost her position in the household and could not be content."

Heft's amusement was wearing thin. "I don't see the point of..."

Olivia raised her voice to over-ride his interruption. "For some months, the situation deteriorated slowly. The sister packed her bag to leave, then decided to stay. But the luggage remained at the foot of the stairs, ready for a sudden hardening of her resolve. And then ...

"One night, the brother -- who occasionally worked at night -- left the cottage in early evening to see a film and go on to his job. The sister, unwilling to stay alone in the house with her rival, went to stay with a friend across town. Then, as sometimes happens in the stories, a coincidence took place."

"Olivia," Heft said, "this had better be good."

"The woman from the city had been associated with the world of theater. Into the village that night drove a man who had been her lover. The woman had expected never to see him again -- he was supposed to have flown to a faraway country. But the trip was postponed and the man came looking for the woman he loved."

"Don't tell me this..."

"They made love, the actor and the woman. It was like the coda following a great symphony -- brief but intense. The event might have remained her secret had not the sister come home in the middle of the night. There had been a family quarrel at the friend's house, she decided to get away."

"Is this why ...?"

"Shhhhh. The sister was appalled. She claimed her packed bag from the foot of the stairs. She told the city woman, 'I'm off. I love my brother too much to stay and see him humiliated. Because I know you will bring him down one day.'"

"I spoke to her on the telephone. I knew something was wrong. She could have scuppered you, but she refused to hurt my feelings."

"The actor sensed tension in the house. He asked questions, he had heard about the brother's fortune made from films. He began suggesting ways of getting hold of that money. One of the ways involved murder."

Heft laughed out loud. "Do you expect me to believe this? Where is your machiavellian lover?"

Olivia got up from the settee. She went to the carafe on its warming stand and poured herself more coffee. She carried her cup to the window and looked out at the garden, at moonlit shrubs, the silhouetted sundial, the dark rank of sunflowers in their bed of recently-turned earth. "The woman knew the actor's potential for wickedness. He was ready for blackmail, possibly for murder. She ordered him to leave the house. He laughed at her. They fought. She pushed him off balance, he fell and struck his head on the sharp edge of a table."

Heft stared at the marble coffee table. He had nothing more to say.

"The man was dead. The woman remained calm. It might yet be for the best. She had plenty of time, she would be alone for hours. She cleared a patch of clover and dug a shallow grave. She managed to drag the body to the hole and cover it over. The extra earth, she scattered among the other plants.

"If I'm to believe you, Olivia, you've killed a man. One of that troupe, The Hartfield Players. Good Lord, this goes back a couple of months to when Pauline disappeared. I suspected somebody was buried in the garden but I thought it was my sister. I've been afraid to call Toronto in case I heard she wasn't there."

"Let me end the story. For weeks, the woman tried to forget that night. She tried to recapture her hold on the quiet life. It seemed to be working. Then ..."

"The pregnancy," Heft said. "Damn you, Olivia. You're carrying his baby." He got up and slammed his cup and saucer on the sideboard. "And I know something else. You aren't going to have an abortion. You're off to New York to have this man's child. I know you."

"Better than I know myself," she said.

For a week after Olivia's departure, Bernard Heft could not bring himself even to step through the kitchen doorway into the back garden. He thought of calling the police but decided against it. The bad actor was dead. He deserved to die, as far as Heft was concerned. If they came and dug up a body in his garden, and the man was identified, then the best he could hope for was that he would be laughed at as a cuckold. At worst, he might be accused of murder.

The decision to dig overcame Heft when it occurred to him that Olivia's story might not be the whole truth and nothing but the truth. She had admitted embellishing some of her earlier efforts. Who was to say this one was entirely factual?

The rivetting suspicion, the one that got Heft into the gardening shed searching for a spade, was the idea that the body might not be that of the actor. He could well have been in New York all this time, waiting for Olivia to show. The corpse under the sunflowers could be Pauline. His dear sister had caught them at it. And they had killed her.

Stand by the police. But first, Heft had to make sure. He uprooted the giant plants and flung them aside. He turned earth, sinking a trench, easy going in dry soil. Down two feet. Three. Had she not said a shallow grave? The ground turned to clay; no shovel had dug here recently, if ever.

Heft stopped digging and began thinking. There was no body in the ground. There had been no murder. Despite himself, he began to laugh.

Inside, with one beer down and another sparkling in the glass, he shook his head in admiration. What a story-teller! But why give him the gory details in a believable framework when it was not true?

Could be she was entertaining him. Or ... maybe the actor had been here and Olivia, feeling guilty, had invented the crime to punish herself and to rule out any chance of Heft coming after her.

The telephone rang and, as if engineered to fit into a Heft scenario, it was Pauline calling from Toronto. "I promised myself to keep out of your life, Bernie. But I have to know how you are."

"Olivia checked out." He told the story, leaving out the pregnancy. "I assume it's true about the actor."

"I'm so glad I don't have to break it to you. It was that good-looking slob from the touring company. I saw him in a couple of things at the high school. Morris Carrington."

"That was my guess. Anyway, do you feel like coming back, Paulie?"

"I'd love to, but I've gone back with Peter. I think we're going to make it work." Her cheerfulness was excessive. "It seems that bitch did me a favor after all."

*   *   *   *   *

Bernard Heft hardly wrote a line for the next five years. It could not have mattered less. His percentage from both films kept filtering down at a rate slightly ahead of what he could spend. He worked on his garden, sang in the church choir, travelled overseas to escape the Baytown winters, dated a kind lady who liked him and shared his enjoyment of movie revivals. As for the Coronet Hotel, he retired at last from that unnecessary job and the entire staff attended his farewell party. But the hotel-owner, Jack Danforth, kept in touch because he had always thought of Bernard Heft as something more than an employee. And the writer continued to eat from time to time in the hotel dining room.

"Take a look at this," Danforth said one day as he sat down at Heft's table and slid a glossy magazine in front of him. He indicated a news photograph of people on a city street. "Isn't that our friend from the trashy show-folk?"

It was indeed. Heft saw a plump, prosperous-looking Olivia Darkling beside the handsome figure of Morris Carrington. Both were indentified in the caption as one of the more successful couples on the New York theater scene with their own production in its third month of packed houses. The description continued; "With the proud pair is their son Clive, aged five years. A chip off the old block?"

Heft looked again and saw the lad almost lost at his father's side. No chip, he. Not off *that* block. The sensitive face peering out at Heft from the magazine page was none other than his own.

"You're laughing," Danforth said. "Why are you laughing?"

"I haven't a clear idea," the writer said. "If I think of one, I'll tell you."

He skipped dessert. He drove home by the shortest route. He went into his study and uncovered the neglected typewriter. There was one more story to tell. He cranked a clean sheet of paper into the machine and began typing as if the words, forced to remain inside, would hurt him.

Tony Aspler

Tony Aspler is known to most people as an
award winning wine writer. But his experience is
just as great in the field of crime writing. A
founding menber of the Crime Writers of Canada,
he was its initial Chairman and the first recipient
of the Derrick Murdoch Award in 1984, for outstanding contributions to the genre in Canada.
His thrillers include *The Music Wars* (1982),
The Scorpion Sanction (1981) and a new mystery
called *Titanic: A Novel* . To be published in the
fall of 1989. He combined both wine and crime
in "Murder by Half", his Atrthur Ellis Award
nominated short story, originally published in
COLD BLOOD: Murder in Canada. "The Year of
the Dragon", however, offers something very different. Wine is replaced with a tattoo artist's
engraved images under a sailor's skin.

THE YEAR OF THE DRAGON

by Tony Aspler

Sailors usually won't admit it, but we get tattooed when we're lonely in a foreign port.

And a little bit drunk. You have to be a little bit drunk to stand the pain.

Tattoos are accidents like wounds, something that happens to you when there are no women around. I know because I have a dragon on my back. It was done by a man in Toronto's Chinatown after a woman had walked out on me.

One sticky summer in 1976 our ship was forced to tie up on the lakeshore because of a stevedores' strike in New York. The owners said we had to wait it out in Canada instead of returning with an empty hold to our home port of Amsterdam.

A bunch of us went into town the first night to tour the bars. When I got talking to a woman they left me behind. I was fascinated by her ears. Instead of earrings she had tiny blue butterflies tattooed to her lobes. They looked so real with their irridescent wings you'd think they would fly away if you touched them.

I asked her where she had them done. She told me about a Chinese tattooist who worked above a restaurant on Gerrard Street. She said his name was Mr. Wha and she showed me the back of her left lobe where he had signed his name. A true artist proud of his work.

I bought her a few drinks and then she told me she had to get home to her husband. I had nothing else to do so I went looking for this man who could paint butterflies on a woman's flesh that made you want to reach out and touch them.

I found the restaurant she mentioned in a rash of old brick buildings. There was a sign in the doorway next to it written in Chinese. Underneath it said in English: "Tattoo Upstairs."

The stairwell was dark and smelled of grease and garlic. I hesitated and was about to turn around and walk out into the street when a light came on above me.

"Come up, please," said a voice that sounded like a flute.

I climbed the stairs and saw a man kneeling on a carpet in the centre of a darkened room. He was dressed in a white shirt, baggy trousers and leather sandals. By his side was a block of wood bristling with bamboo canes. Next to it were egg cups set on a plastic tray. Each was filled with a different colour. A bright light hung above his head throwing the rest of the room into deep shadow.

"I am Mr. Wha. You have come to have your body painted."

He made it sound more like a statement than a question. The ageless face, the colour of putty, looked up at me and smiled.

"Please take off your shirt."

He rose to his feet and began examining my skin. He ran his fingers over my shoulders. His touch was as gentle as a woman's but his wrists were thick and muscular like a weight-lifter's.

"What does your skin feel it needs?" he asked.

I shrugged, not knowing what design I wanted.

"Haven't you got any pictures I could choose from?"

I felt myself swaying. The effects of the whisky I had drunk and the overpowering smell of garlic made the room spin.

"You are not ready," he said. "Come back when you feel your body is a canvas."

From the shadows another voice called out something in Chinese, harsh and threatening. I peered into the darkness and dimly made out the figure of another man seated quite still in the corner.

Mr. Wha sighed.

"This is The Year of the Dragon and that is what you will have. The Dragon is the King of the Seas."

The other man said something else in Chinese and Mr. Wha clicked his tongue.

"It will cost $100, please. In advance."

He held out his hand. I reached into my pocket and felt for five $20 bills. I handed them to him but before he could take the money the other man snatched it and moved to another room. In the light I caught sight of his eyes. They were black and menacing, the blackest eyes I had ever seen.

Mr. Wha motioned me to lie down on the floor. The carpet smelled dusty and I turned my head towards the kneeling artist so that I could watch him work.

He opened a straight razor and began to strop it expertly on a leather. He drew the blade over my back, explaining that he had to remove the hair. Then he reached for a rag, dipped it into a colourless liquid and began to rub it all over my back.

"Alcohol," he said. "Everything will be clean. You will heal quickly."

He selected a bamboo cane and inspected the long needle sticking out of the end. First he dipped it into the alcohol and then into the tiny pool of red paint. With his left thumb and forefinger he spread the skin on my shoulder tight and held the needle poised over it. He shut his eyes and his lips moved without sound. He remained in this position for a full minute before he opened his eyes again and brought the needle down, piercing my skin.

His wrist worked as quickly as a sewing machine, each tiny point of pain becoming a dot of colour which spread into a line.

For two hours I lay there wondering what he was doing and when he rose I asked for a mirror.

"I have not finished," he said. "You must come back every day until it is captured."

"But my ship could sail any day," I protested. "I want it finished now."

Mr. Wha shook his head.

"You cannot rush a dragon. I am coaxing it out of your flesh. Out of your muscles and sinews. It will appear when it is ready. You must let me finish. Come to me tomorrow," he said.

He showed me to the door and bowed.

I returned the next day as soon as I got off duty. Mr. Wha was waiting for me, kneeling on the carpet as I had first seen him. He smiled when I came in.

"It looks great," I said, as I took off my shirt and lay down on the floor.

"You should not look at it until it is finished," he chided me.

For five days I returned to Mr. Wha and each day I learned a little more about him. He was an artist in Hong Kong and had come to Canada with his wife and young son to join his older brother who owned the restaurant downstairs. He helped to support his family by his tattooing. His wife worked in the kitchen. "Long hours," he said, with distaste, and I got the feeling that life in Toronto was hard for him.

Once his son came upstairs to watch his father at work, admiring the way he manipulated the needles. The boy said nothing to me but I saw in his eyes the respect and love he had for his father.

Mr. Wha's brother put his head around the door from time to time, to see how the work was progressing. He ignored me completely as if I were a wall on which his brother was painting a mural.

My shipmates began to wonder where I went each day. They joked that I was with the butterfly woman. I didn't want to show them my dragon until Mr. Wha said he was satisfied. I felt that somehow I would be betraying the artist to take my shirt off in front of my bunk-mates just yet.

I was glad that the stevedore strike allowed me to visit Mr. Wha each day. I would lie on the floor for two hours while he breathed fire into the dragon on my back. He could only work for two hours, he said, because his wrist tired after that.

In spite of the pain of the needles, I felt at peace in his

presence. He explained to me how he applied the colours and how he used the contours of my back in his design. Occasionally, he would ask me to flex my muscles.

When he finished he had me stand up with my back to a full-length mirror. He handed me a small looking glass so that I could see the reflection without having to contort my body.

The left side of my back, from the waist up to the shoulder, was filled with a whirling red and yellow five-clawed dragon. Its terrible black eyes were the eyes of Mr. Wha's brother. The dragon breathed with me. When I moved it moved, its scales shimmering in the light. When I flexed my muscles its jaws opened, its belly swelled and it really looked as if it breathed fire.

"Now you are a dragon," he said, "and every dragon has a story."

"It's wonderful, Mr. Wha. It's alive."

Mr Wha looked frightened and he hauled me to my feet, handing me my shirt.

"You must go now," he said.

There were tears running down his face.

When I returned to the ship I was summoned before the Captain. He had received orders to sail home immediately. All hands had been called back on board and I was not at my post. I explained why I was late and took off my shirt to show him.

The Captain studied my back in amazement. He said he had never seen anything like it in all his years at sea. He was so intrigued he forgot to discipline me.

"The guy even signed it," he said, "like a real artist."

And sure enough, there were Chinese characters under the dragon's tail that coiled around above my kidneys.

Mr. Wha had told me that the colours would remain as bright and vivid as they were now until the next Year of the Dragon came round.

I made a vow that twelve years later I would return to Toronto to show him the dragon he had "coaxed" from my flesh. Perhaps he could do another picture for me on my right side.

*   *   *   *   *

The Gerrard Street restaurant was still there and so was the doorway leading up to the room above. But there was a new sign now. "Tattoo Parlour -- Expert body painting," it read.

I walked up the stairs. Twelve years had not dissipated the smell of grease and garlic which seemed to ooze from the newly painted walls. I knocked on the door. A young Chinese opened it and I recognised the face of Mr. Wha's son, now grown to manhood.

The room was brightly painted and the walls were hung with various designs of fish and birds and serpents. In the centre was a chair that resembled something you'd see in a dentist's office. Next to it was a table with electrical tools and wires running into a switch box.

"I'm looking for Mr. Wha," I said.

The young man's face remained expressionless.

"I am Mr. Wha."

"No, your father."

"My father has been dead for many years," he said.

"I'm sorry to hear that. He made me a beautiful tattoo. I wanted to show him how well it's lasted."

"May I see it?"

I removed my jacket and shirt and hung them on the back of the door. Then I stood with my back to the mirror. As soon as he saw the red and yellow dragon, the young man nodded his head.

"I remember."

He moved closer to me to study the design. I glanced at his face in the mirror and could see his expression soften. It was the same look he wore while he had watched his father creating the design.

He put his fingertips on the head of the dragon and traced its curving line down my back.

Suddenly, he pulled away as if my body had given him an electric shock. He started shaking and hurried into the next room. No sooner had he disappeared than he was back again, dragging a middle-aged woman behind him.

She wiped her hands on her apron, protesting in Chinese as she came.

The young man turned me around and pointed to my back. She leaned in for a closer look. Then she too drew back in horror and fled into the room from which she had just been dragged.

"What the hell's going on?" I demanded.

The young man regained his composure and asked me to lie face down in the chair.

"Why?" I asked.

"The tattoo needs refreshing. It is my father's work but it is very old. I will do it for nothing. In memory of my father."

Puzzled, I sat down and the young man began to apply oil to my back.

"What are you doing?" I asked.

"First," he said, "I must remove my father's name."

"No," I said. "I don't want it taken off."

"But the moment I work on it it is no longer his."

"It's a work of art," I replied. "You don't take Van Gogh's name off a painting just because you're getting it restored."

"But you do not understand. In our culture a man who paints another man's body must not leave his name there."

I rose from the chair and pushed him aside, grabbing my shirt and jacket as I made for the door.

"I'm proud to have your father's name on my back," I shouted. "And if you had any respect for his memory you'd leave it there."

The young man stood in the middle of the room shaking as I slammed the door on my way downstairs.

I walked the Toronto streets thinking about Mr. Wha and his son who had followed in his footsteps but had abandoned the old methods. Why did he want to erase his father's name? And why had the woman, who was obviously Mr. Wha's widow, reacted the way she did?

At times like this, when you're alone in a foreign city, you return to familiar places. I sought out the bar where I had met the woman with butterfly ears twelve years ago. It had changed little but I was not interested in the surroundings. I just sat in a booth, drinking whisky after whisky, remembering the feel of the needles in my back and Mr. Wha's soothng, flute-like voice.

It was dark when I called for the check. I reached for the wallet in my inside pocket but it was not there. Surely Mr. Wha's son would not have stolen it. It must have dropped out when I snatched my jacket from the hook.

I explained the situation to the bored waiter who accepted my watch by way of payment. A Rolex I had bought in Singapore. I told him I would redeem it as soon as I picked up my wallet from the Tattoo Parlour.

I raced back to Gerrard Street to find that the sidewalk outside the restaurant had been cordoned off with fluorescent orange tape. A policeman stood in the doorway to the upstairs rooms.

"I'm sorry, sir," he said, "No one's allowed up there."

"What happened?" I asked.

"Police business, sir."

"But I was just here, a few hours ago."

The policeman suddenly became interested in me.

"Is that so? If you wouldn't mind coming upstairs with me, sir."

He held my elbow as he ushered me up the stairs.

The room was swarming with men. Some were in uniform; others in civilian dress, dusting surfaces for fingerprints. The dentist's chair was draped with a sheet. In the adjoining room I could hear the sound of a woman sobbing.

"This gentleman says he was here earlier today, Inspector Chou."

He was addressing a Chinese man in a blue lounge suit. At first I was surprised to see a Chinese detective heading an investigation but it made perfect sense. A crime committed in Chinatown. Who better to understand the workings of a tight-knit community that keeps itself to itself.

"Ah, you must be the owner of this."

He held up a plastic bag which contained my black leather wallet. I put out my hand but he drew it away from me.

"You have saved me a great deal of trouble by returning for it."

He beckoned me closer to the chair and pulled back the sheet. Lying there was Mr. Wha's brother, his staring black eyes as menacing in death as they had been in life.

A bamboo cane protruded from his right ear. A trickle of blood had dried on his neck.

"Do you know this man?"

"I saw him twelve years ago when I had my tattoo done."

The detective frowned.

"I must warn you that anything you say will be taken down and may be used in evidence against you."

For one moment I thought he was joking. How many times had I heard the same words in cheap movie houses?

"But I don't know anything about this," I protested. "I just came back for my wallet."

Inspector Chou continued to watch me. I could feel the dragon on my back. Its scales twitched and shivered; they seemed to slide over each other beneath the sheen of my perspiration. The police thought I had killed him.

"Look, you can check with the bar down the street. I was there all afternoon. I had to leave my watch because I couldn't pay. You have my money in my wallet there."

I could hear the desperation in my voice. Yet I felt compelled to keep talking.

"I didn't kill him, I tell you."

"Who did you see here?"

"I saw Mr. Wha's son and a woman who looked like his mother."

"And why did you come this afternoon?"

"I came to show Mr. Wha the tattoo he did twelve years ago. I had no idea he had died."

"Why did you leave your wallet behind?"

"Because I left in a hurry."

"Why?"

"The man, Mr. Wha's son, wanted to change the tattoo his father had done. I got angry so I left. But I never touched anyone."

The detective replaced the sheet over the corpse's face.

"Before we fingerprint you, may I see the tattoo, please?"

I felt awkward taking off my shirt in front of a room full of policemen.

"Please be so kind as to step to the window," said Inspector Chou.

His voice seemed to purr with suspicion.

The red and yellow dragon reared in the glow of the streetlights outside. I could see the inspector's eyes open in admiration. He called one of his associates over and together they scrutinised my back, talking softly in Chinese. Then he called to the photographer and directed him to take pictures of my tattoo.

"When did you say you had this done?" asked the Inspector.

"I told you. Twelve years ago," I replied. "Mr. Wha signed it but I don't know if he put the date. I don't read Chinese."

The two men conferred again and the Inspector asked me to accompany him to the police station to make a statement.

In the car, he questioned me about the dead man, Mr. Wha, his wife and his son. I told him the little I remembered of my conversations with the artist.

When we arrived at Police Headquarters he showed me into a room and asked me to wait. Eventually, he returned with another photographer.

"We would like to take some more pictures. If you would kindly remove your shirt again."

"I would like to contact a lawyer," I said, although I knew no-one in Toronto, let alone a lawyer.

Inspector Chou rubbed the tips of his fingers together and looked sad.

"All in good time."

"But why am I here? I had nothing to do with this," I protested again.

Inspector Chou whispered something to his associate and then turned back to me.

"I'm prepared to believe that," he said.

"Then you have no right to hold me."

"I'm sorry, sir. We know who killed the man you identified. What we didn't know was why. Until you came. You are -- how shall I put this? You are the link."

"What are you talking about?"

"The artist who drew that remarkable dragon on your back created more than a work of art. He also made a diary. Where each scale connects he drew word pictures."

"What did he say?"

"Turn around and I will read it to you."

"It says: 'My wife works hard. She resists my brother Chi's advances. I know he will kill me tonight. I see it in his eyes.'"

The words Mr. Wha spoke twelve years ago suddenly came back to me. "Now you are a dragon and every dragon has a story."